Trinitarian Perspectives in the Franciscan Theological Tradition

Maria Calisi

VOLUME FIVE
THE FRANCISCAN HERITAGE SERIES

CFIT / ESC-OFM
2008

© The Franciscan Institute
St. Bonaventure University
St. Bonaventure, NY 14778
2008

This pamphlet is the fifth in
The Franciscan Heritage Series
sponsored by the
Commission on the Franciscan Intellectual Tradition
of the English-speaking Conference of the
Order of Friars Minor
(CFIT/ESC-OFM)

General Editor
Joseph P. Chinnici, O.F.M.

Assistant Editor
Daria Mitchell, O.S.F.

ISBN: 978-1-57659-2045

Library of Congress Control Number: 2008940403

Printed and bound in the United States of America
BookMasters, Inc.
Ashland, Ohio

TABLE OF CONTENTS

Abbreviations	5
General Editor's Introduction:	7
Author's Introduction: The Scriptural Revelation and Trinitarian Theology	15

PART I:
BONAVENTURE'S TRINITARIAN THEOLOGY — 19

Eastern and Western Trinitarian Theologies	19
The Father's Primacy Understood as Fecundity	21
The Self-Diffusiveness of the Good	23
Bonaventure and Richard of St. Victor	27
Bonaventure and Greek Patristic Trinitarian Theology	31
Bonaventure and Process Theology	34
Bonaventure's Doctrine of Exemplarity	35
The Son	39
The Son as Image and Word	40
Christocentricity	43
In Whom All Things Hold Together	46
The Holy Spirit	47
The *Filioque*	48
The Highest Self-communication	50
The *Filioque* and the History of Salvation	51
The *Filioque* and the *Persona Media*	53

The Distinction between the Son and the Spirit	53
The Unity of the Trinity: The Single Divine Nature	54
Each Person Unifies the Trinity	55
Circumincession	56

Bonaventure:
  The Franciscan Resource for Theological Questions Today   59

PART II:
BONAVENTURE, FRANCIS, AND THE EXPERIENCE OF THE TRI-PERSONAL GOD   63

Introduction	63
Bonaventure's *Major Legend* of Saint Francis	65
Francis's Own Writings	68
Primacy of the Father	71
The Son as the Word and Central Person of the Trinity	74
The Trinity and the Eucharist	77
The Holy Spirit: Our Inspiration and Unity	80
Conclusion	86

About the Author

Maria Calisi received her PhD., M.A., and B.A., from Fordham University. She currently serves as Assistant Professor, Chairperson of the Department of Theology, St. Peter's College, New Jersey.

ABBREVIATIONS

The following abbreviations are used in the text to designate writings of Francis and early biographical sources for the life of Francis. Unless otherwise indicated, all references are from *Francis of Assisi: Early Documents*, three volumes, ed. Regis J. Armstrong, J.A. Wayne Hellmann, William J. Short (New York: New City Press: 1999, 2000, 2001). The abbreviations designating the writings of Clare and early biographical sources for the life of Clare are taken from *Clare of Assisi Early Documents, The Lady*, ed. and trans. Regis J. Armstrong, (New York, New City Press: 2006).

FAED	*Francis of Assisi: Early Documents*, vols. 1-3 (New York: New City Press)
FC	Fathers of the Church Series (Washington: CUA Press)
FHS	Franciscan Heritage Series, Commission on the Franciscan Intellectual Tradition (St. Bonaventure, NY: Franciscan Institute Publications)
NPNF	Nicene and Post-Nicene Fathers (Grand Rapids: Eerdmans)
WSB	Works of St. Bonaventure (St. Bonaventure, NY: Franciscan Institute Publications)

GENERAL EDITOR'S INTRODUCTION

Trinitarian Perspectives in the Franciscan Theological Tradition by Dr. Maria Calisi builds substantially on the previous four volumes in the *Franciscan Heritage Series* sponsored by the Secretariat for the Retrieval of the Franciscan Intellectual Tradition (CFIT) of the English Speaking Conference of the Order of Friars Minor. Dr. Calisi is an authority on the theology of Saint Bonaventure. Her exposition of the foundations of the Seraphic Doctor's theology in the contemplative experience of and reflection on the relational nature of God's life retrieves an important theological perspective applicable to our contemporary search for meaning. Well schooled in the patristic inheritance, familiar with the riches of Orthodox theology, knowledgeable in the writings of Francis himself, Dr. Calisi engages the reader with a simple but profound analysis of the creedal sign shared by all Christians: "In the name of the Father, the Son, and the Holy Spirit." In these pages we will discover how doctrine can shape life, and life, doctrine; how faith-filled human beings rooted in Trinitarian love can bear great fruit for both Church and society by engaging practitioners in action supportive of personal dignity, ecumenical relationships, social transformation, and ecclesial reform.

It is with great pleasure and gratitude that the sponsors of CFIT offer this reflection to a wider public. Previous volumes have presented an overview of the tradition, discussed dimensions of creation and Christian anthropology in Franciscan theology, and illustrated them through an iconographic tradition founded in the Gospel of John. It is our hope that *Trinitarian Perspectives in the Franciscan Theological Tradition* will present in an accessible and exciting form the central foundational element of the theological vision to students in the college classroom, the parish adult education program, Secular Fraternity gatherings, and various community meetings. Oftentimes in the history of Christianity the exposition of our Trinitarian belief has been confined simply to the realm of an incomprehensible and somewhat irrelevant "mystery" far removed from the concerns of ordinary life. Such is not the case in a world shaped by the sundering of relationships and the longing for belonging. The depth of the presentation and its consequences for our life will only be plumbed through a process of intellectual and affective conversion: If we believe that God is three-in-one, what does it mean to be "made in God's image"? If we recognize that the social nature of God is foundational to our own quest for happiness, what structures can we create so as to anticipate this celestial economy of exchange *in via*? If we are to practice what we believe, how can we recommit ourselves to the creation of loving ecclesial relationships, to the treasuring of the revelation of God's relational being in all of creation? May the grace of our Lord Jesus Christ, the love of God, and the fellowship of the Holy Spirit guide us in this task.

A Unique Franciscan Vision

The foundational significance of *Trinitarian Perspectives in the Franciscan Theological Tradition* may be seen by approaching the reading with the anthropological question in the back of one's mind: What does it mean to be human in today's Church and world? This has been explored initially in the third book in the *Heritage* series *A Franciscan View of the Human Person* (2005), and here only a few areas need be mentioned to indicate how this current exposition might be further explored and applied. Calisi indicates some other implications at the end of her exposition on Bonaventure.

Today in our world we all seek for happiness, an end to violence, a resting place of plenty, a clear knowledge of that which is true. We all search for goodness. "Everything," Bonaventure writes, "naturally tends toward its source. A stone tends downward; fire tends upward; rivers run to the sea; the tree is joined to its root, and other things are joined to their roots. The rational creature is God-like."[1] In other words, by our nature we tend towards home, the relationships from which we came, the weight of our desire and love leading us towards complete happiness. For Bonaventure, as a Christian, communion with God, with others, and with all of creation is our human destination. What great happiness would ensue were we to find our complete rest not in the possession of an infinite number of things, a poor consumer substitute for the focus of an infinite desire – although all of these material things may be good, but in Someone capable of fulfilling our heart's desire for personal communion, love, peace, plenty, immortality. When describing "beatitude" as a final resting place Bonaventure identifies many elements that make this goal real. Among them are: "a handsome and noble servant to serve you; there is savory and tasty food to refresh you; likeable and most friendly companions to rejoice with you."[2] These are all gifts conferred gratuitously by a generous God. And as a true Augustinian, Bonaventure had great confidence in the original "potency" in us which makes us "capable of cleaving to him whose image" we are.[3] The question becomes, if God is our origin and our end, if we come from the One who is Good and are going to the one who is Good, how do we image God in both our minds and in our actions?

Maria Calisi in this work makes the Franciscan image of God as Good, as expressed by Bonaventure, abundantly evident. As he writes in the *Breviloquium*, and she analyzes with precision and scholarly clarity in its distinctiveness, God is not only "supreme unity, infinity, eternity, immutability necessity, and sovereign primacy," but also "highest fecundity, love gen-

---

[1] Bonaventure of Bagnoregio, *Collations on the Seven Gifts of the Holy Spirit*, III: 5, trans. Zachary F. Hayes, O.F.M., Works of St. Bonaventure XIV (St. Bonaventure, New York: Franciscan Institute Publications, 2008), 68-69.

[2] Bonaventure of Bagnoregio, "On the Perfection of Life," VIII: 3, in *Writings on the Spiritual Life*, Introduction and Notes by F. Edward Coughlin, trans. Girard Etzkorn, Works of St. Bonaventure X (St. Bonaventure, New York: Franciscan Institute Publications, 2006), 191.

[3] Augustine, *De Trinitate*, XIV.4:20, *The Trinity*, WSA 5, introduction, translation and notes Edmund Hill, O.P., ed. John E. Rotelle, O.S.A., (New York: New City Press, 1991), 386.

erosity, equality, relationship, likeness, and inseparability."[4] This focus is different from that of Thomas Aquinas. When examining the question of a plurality of persons in God, Thomas struggles to reconcile the inherited definition of person with the unity of God's divine nature.[5] Bonaventure's response seems much more alive, and dynamic, more relational, more human.[6] To paraphrase, he focuses on God's happiness: Where there is supreme happiness, there is supreme goodness, supreme charity, supreme joyfulness. And how can there be goodness unless there is supreme self-communication, generating from oneself another who is equal and giving him being? And how can one have charity, since charity is not a private love, unless one has charity towards another? And how can one have joy without a companion? Supreme joy requires a society and therefore a plurality of persons! Here we have an image of God – good, loving, joyful – to be reflected in we who are made in God's image and redeemed by God's own Image, a picture of ultimate reality which dictates a practical social ethic: poverty and humility in the giving of self and treating others as equals, charity in turning towards another, joyfulness in the presence of the companion. Here is a Franciscan way of being present in the world so as to proclaim in word and deed a human experience of God as love. The call of our Christian and Franciscan life is with God's grace in Christ to become deiform. This is a blessed and liberating faith that comes to us through the Church. Placing the Trinity at the center of our prayer and practice changes how we might be in the world. It is a topic that begs for further exploration, but by exposing the riches of Bonaventurian teaching, Dr. Calisi has pointed us in the right direction.

It has often struck me that this particular emphasis on the Trinity as Goodness, Charity, and Joyfulness with its accompanying ethical call may be the most timely image of God which

---

[4] Bonaventure of Bagnoregio, *Breviloquium*, 2:2, Works of St. Bonaventure IX, Trans. by Dominic Monti (St. Bonaventure, NY: Franciscan Institute Publications, 2005), 30.

[5] Thomas of Aquinas, *Summa Theologica*, I, q30, a1

[6] Bonaventure of Bagnoregio, *Commentary on the Sentences*, I *Sent.* d2, a1, q2).

can be presented in today's world. Part of the Franciscan spiritual inheritance, the vision of God as self-diffusive goodness is foundational for the Christian calling in a violent and fragmented society. In his *Collations on the Seven Gifts of the Holy Spirit*, Bonaventure writes in reference to both Church and society:

> Today there is such great cruelty that a person cannot be satisfied with vengeance. Today impatience and anger rule. People pass evil judgments. Even if a person has not offended me, I will still attribute evil to him. Why is this? Certainly it is because I do not have charity.[7]

The remedy for this situation that Bonaventure identifies is the worship of the Most High expressed in *pietas*, itself a chief characteristic of the Triune God. Piety resides in the middle, between patience and charity. It is a healing medicine for wayfarers who are wounded. An understanding of piety evolves from its embodiment: "No brother [or sister], I could not lead you to the original sources of piety except through the act and the exercise of piety."[8] In other words, the life of the Triune God is learned through practice. What are the practical implications for life when belief in the Trinity expressed in the sign of the cross is the mark of what it means to be, as a Christian, a full, good, joyful and generous human being with other human beings?

Focusing on the Trinity, a dynamic and fecund society of persons in complete self-giving (cf. Calisi on *circumincession*) so much so that there is only One God, distinction and unity given simultaneously, places belief in Love and its power at the center of the Franciscan vision. This has implications for the path practitioners might choose to order the ecclesial and social world in which they live. Never perfectly ordering the world the way God is, they nonetheless avoid certain negatives and develop certain pathways which give witness to the primacy of God's order. The options are many: control the chaos of the world through ideological absolutes, retreat into enclaves

---

[7] St. Bonaventure, *Collations*, III:9, WSB XIV, 74.
[8] St. Bonaventure, *Collations*, III:10, WSB XIV, 74.

of security, a will to domination and power through money or military might, an insistence on legal prescriptions, positional authority, self-referential interpretations of the past. In his *Disputed Questions on Evangelical Perfection*, Bonaventure argues for the practice of humility as "the foundation of all Christian perfection."[9] Some object that such a practice of humility would destroy hierarchical order: "When a superior subjects himself to an inferior, then there are disorder and a perversion of order."[10] The Seraphic Doctor responds with a quintessential Franciscan answer based on the logic of Trinitarian life:

> ... it must be said that the order of love that is attained in virtue has this principally, radically, and essentially in view: God is preferred to the creature. Every other order is connected and ordered to the divine order as its principal order.[11]

The one who acts most contrary to this Trinitarian order is the one who clings to a private good. Yet when life is ordered through a Trinitarian practice then

> an individual subjects himself to another and places someone else ahead of himself for the sake of God, guarding all the while the dignity of ecclesiastical order which true humility does not pervert, neglect, or relegate to a secondary position.[12]

A Franciscan Trinitarian perspective in prayer and practice issues in a mission for all Christians to reform Church and society.

---

[9] Bonaventure of Bagnoregio, *Disputed Questions on Evangelical Perfection*, Q I, conclusion, Works of St. Bonaventure XIII, Introduction and Notes by Fr. Robert J. Karris (St. Bonaventure, New York: Franciscan Institute Publications, 2008), 40.

[10] St. Bonaventure, *Disputed Questions*, Neg.2, WSB XIII, 37.

[11] St. Bonaventure, *Disputed Questions*, Replies to Neg.2, WSB XIII, 48-49.

[12] St. Bonaventure, *Disputed Questions*, Replies to Neg.2, WSB XIII, 49.

Making Connections

The great Dominican medievalist M.-D. Chenu once remarked, "a theology worthy of the name is a spirituality which has found rational instruments adequate to its religious experience." Calisi's Trinitarian Perspectives, by beginning with an exposition of Bonaventure's theology of God, and then moving towards an examination of Francis's own experience as expressed in his writings, shows clearly how a spirituality handed down in prayers, *legendae*, religious practices, and an oral tradition of spiritual wisdom comes to take expression in another language, that of the academic schools. She has reversed the chronological order so as to demonstrate a continuity in the spiritual order. Some might argue with this approach, choosing to emphasize instead Bonaventure's discontinuity with Francis. As members of the CFIT commission reviewed the question, we recognized the difficulties but considered it a methodology worth pondering. Bonaventure's theology thus becomes constructive in a new way and traditional in an old way. Perhaps there is in the uniqueness of Francis and Bonaventure a still discernible and fundamental continuity. Perhaps the Seraphic Doctor has become the scribe of the Gospels, "who brings from his storeroom both the new and the old" (Matt 13:52). Is this not what we are called to do today? Can there not be new Bonaventures laboring to retrieve the old so as to make all things new?

The Franciscan Intellectual Tradition Project

In March, 2001, the English-speaking Conference, Order of Friars Minor, undertook an initiative for the contemporary retrieval of the Franciscan Intellectual Tradition. Composed of the leaders of the provinces and other entities of England, Ireland, Canada, and the United States, the Conference established an inter-obediential commission to facilitate the coordination and networking of various publications and popular initiatives that were already taking place throughout the English-speaking world. As one of its first initiatives, this Commission for the Retrieval of the Franciscan Intellectual Tradition (CFIT) composed and published a strategic five-year plan and working document on the major themes of the theological and social vision. These initial plans and enunciation of the vision are available at the website *Franciscantradition.org*. The initiative has taken specific shape through the publication of the academic papers of an annual symposium at The Washington Theological Union. *The Heritage Series*, now numbering five volumes, is designed to communicate the tradition in a more accessible, shorter, and popular form for use in small groups and study clubs. All of the publications are available through the Franciscan Institute, St. Bonaventure University, St. Bonaventure, New York. In 2007 the Commission for the Retrieval of the Franciscan Intellectual Tradition was reconstituted as a Secretariat of the English Speaking Conference, Order of Friars Minor. Formational work within and without the Franciscan family, networking through the Association of Franciscan Colleges and Universities, the coordination of publishing, the translation of volumes in the *Heritage Series* into French and Spanish, and the development of popular forms of communication through the use of technology and print media have been other parts of CFIT's activity. Most recently the Secretariat has been facilitating the formation of FIAF, Franciscan International Academic Federation, a cooperative program networking four institutions: Pontifical University Antonianum, Rome, Italy; International Franciscan Study Center, Canterbury, England; Franciscan Institute, St. Bonaventure, New York; Franciscan School of Theology, Berkeley, California. Inquiries may be sent to members of the core commission: Father Joseph P. Chinnici, O.F.M., Franciscan School of Theology, 1712 Euclid Ave., Berkeley, California 94708; Sister Margaret Carney, O.S.F., President, or Brother Edward Coughlin, O.F.M., St. Bonaventure University, St. Bonaventure, New York, 14778.

Joseph P. Chinnici, O.F.M.
Franciscan School of Theology

Introduction:
The Scriptural Revelation
and Trinitarian Theology

In those days Jesus came from Nazareth of Galilee and was baptized by John in the Jordan. And when he came up out of the water, immediately he saw the heavens opened and the Spirit descending upon him like a dove; and a voice came from heaven, "Thou art my beloved Son; with thee I am well pleased" (Mark 1:9-11).

When Thou wast baptized in the Jordan, the worship of the Trinity was made manifest. For the voice of the Father bore witness to Thee, calling Thee His beloved Son. And the Spirit, in the form of a dove, confirmed the truthfulness of His word. Oh Christ our God, who hast revealed thyself and enlightened the world, glory to Thee (Troparion of Theophany).[13]

All four of the Gospels present the baptism of Jesus in the Jordan River as the only time God is made manifest as three Persons.[14] This was fitting because Jesus' baptism may be viewed as the inauguration of Jesus' public ministry in which he proclaimed the reign of God. Jesus' revelation was of a God who is boundlessly loving and intensely personal, and who therefore

---

[13] In the Eastern Orthodox Church and in the Eastern Rite of the Catholic Church, a troparion is the hymn for the feast day that is sung in the liturgy. Rather than the word *Epiphany*, *Theophany* is the Orthodox Church's name for the Feast of the Lord's Baptism, because at that event God as a Trinity of Persons was made manifest. The *Epiphany* is the name used in the Western Churches.

[14] Cf. Matt 3:13-17; Mark 1:9-11; Luke 3:21-22; John 1:29-34.

is ever-seeking communion with us. His contemporaries experienced this very God in Jesus of Nazareth; they knew God, felt God, sensed God, encountered God, were forgiven and transformed by God in Jesus, and thereby proclaimed that Jesus is Lord. Yet, this same Jesus related to God as Father and as "other." Jesus spoke about the Father, taught about the Father, loved the Father, and prayed to the Father. In short, he revealed the Father as "another Person." Similarly Jesus spoke of the Holy Spirit as "other;" he was conceived by the Spirit, anointed by the Spirit, empowered by the Spirit, led and driven by the Spirit. Finally, after his resurrection Jesus sent and shared the Spirit. In his exemplary life and teachings, Jesus revealed that God is tri-personal because God is essentially relational. God is relationality itself because God is love.

From its earliest beginnings in Galilee and throughout the centuries, the Christian experience of God has been an experience through a relationship with Christ and in the Spirit. This has been the primordial, perhaps unconscious, experience of God. How are Christians to articulate this experience? How are we to formulate this understanding of who God is in a teaching about God? Trinitarian theology is an attempt to speak as fully as we are able about our relationship with Christ through whom we experience God's love, mercy, community, and salvation; and to speak of our relationship with the Spirit who sustains us, unifies us, inspires us to pray and seek God ever more. Yet, trinitarian theology is also an attempt to articulate an understanding of God "in Godself," that is, to formulate a doctrine about God's nature apart from us. It endeavors to give a reasonable account of how the One God of Israel is also the three Persons of the Father, Son, and Holy Spirit. This latter effort has tended to dominate trinitarian theology, especially in the well-known trinitarian models of Augustine (d. 430) and Thomas Aquinas (d. 1274) in the Western Church, and of the Cappadocian Fathers[15] in the Eastern Orthodox Church.

---

[15] The Cappadocian Fathers are Basil the Great (d. 379), his brother Gregory of Nyssa (d. 394), and his friend Gregory of Nazianzen (d. 390), all of whom wrote extensively on the Trinity.

The purpose of this volume in the Franciscan Heritage Series is to present distinctly Franciscan perspectives on the doctrine of the Trinity in writings of Bonaventure (d. 1274) and Francis (d. 1226), and to demonstrate what this tradition has to offer to the Christian Church. The Franciscan understanding about the Trinity is that it is first, foremost, thoroughly and ultimately a revelation about the infinitely overflowing love of God who is a communion of persons in self-giving relationship.

Rather than beginning chronologically with Francis, it would be more fruitful to look at Bonaventure first, because his theology of the Trinity is highly developed in what can be considered uniquely Franciscan elements. Then it would be easier to identify the same elements in the life and writings of Francis.

Part I: Bonaventure's Trinitarian Theology

Eastern and Western Trinitarian Theologies

Much of Bonaventure's highly developed trinitarian theology is arguably about God in Godself, i.e., about the pre-cosmic and eternal processions, relations, and unity within the inner life of God. This had been part of the scholastic theology that was done at the University of Paris, especially by Thomas Aquinas, during Bonaventure's lifetime in the thirteenth century. However, Bonaventure's theology is not *just* about God in Godself; this would have led to an understanding of the Trinity that is locked up within itself and unrelated to us and all of creation.[16] The Seraphic Doctor strives to understand all of God's activity in the world as the work of the Trinity; that is, creation, Incarnation, redemption, sanctification, and salvation are the work of the Father through the Son in the power of the Spirit. He does not separate his understanding of who God is as a Trinity of Persons from these central Christian teachings. It is on the basis of what Christ revealed in history, especially that God is infinitely overflowing love, that Bonaventure then speculates on the inner life of God and contemplates why God is three Persons: God is tri-Personal because God is love and interper-

---

[16] This Augustinian-Thomistic trinitarian theology has dominated in the Western Church (the Catholic and Protestant Churches) to the extent that the doctrine of the Trinity became divorced from the other Christian teachings such as Christology, soteriology (theology of salvation), theological anthropology, ethics, spirituality, and the doctrine of creation. Karl Rahner's lament is often repeated in trinitarian discourse that the whole doctrine of the Trinity could be eliminated "as false [and] the major part of religious literature could well remain virtually unchanged." Karl Rahner, *The Trinity* (New York: Herder & Herder, 1970), 11.

Walter Kasper is another theologian who thinks we should reunite the doctrine of the Trinity with its Christological origins. Walter Kasper, *The God of Jesus Christ* (New York: Crossroad, 1984).

sonal relationship is necessary for the perfection of love. The centrality of God's love is at the heart of all Franciscan theology and all Franciscan insight. The love of God sets Francis ablaze in following Christ, and this love permeates his whole life and radiates beyond himself to generations of followers. A follower of Francis himself, Bonaventure never loses sight of the central truth of God's love for us and it resonates in all his theology, no matter how speculative or philosophically sophisticated it becomes.

Bonaventure's approach to discussing the Trinity is, for the most part, to begin with the person of the Father, rather than with the divine "substance" or divine being. To begin with the divine substance is a somewhat more abstract and impersonal approach. A "substance" may be defined as "a thing in itself." A "person" may be defined as "one toward another." This is the way that Augustine and Thomas begin their trinitarian discourses, and then they proceed to discuss the divine persons as mutual and opposite relations *within* the Godhead. It is important at the outset that we recognize this difference between beginning with the Father and beginning with the notion of substance.

To be "personal" is to be essentially capable of relationship. To start talking about the Trinity in terms of personhood, rather than substance, is immediately to say that relationality is the nature of God, that the nature of God is love. While almost the entire Western Church understood the doctrine of the Trinity in terms of "substance," is it any wonder that the Franciscan would gravitate to an understanding of the Trinity that starts with interpersonal love?

Bonaventure's starting point of relationality immediately places him in continuity with the Eastern approach to Trinitarian theology. Whereas the Latin Western theology begins with the divine substance, Eastern Orthodox theology or Cappadocian trinitarian theology also begins with the Father. Now considered the classic difference between the Greek and Latin models of the Trinity, these generalizations were devised by

Theodore de Régnon[17] over a hundred years ago. Besides the question of starting points, the models offer different emphases: the Greek model emphasizes personhood more than substance and trineness more than unity, while the Latin model emphasizes the divine substance more than personhood and unity more than trineness. This starting point of relationality, which Bonaventure shares with the Greek tradition, has important implications.

THE FATHER'S PRIMACY UNDERSTOOD AS FECUNDITY

To begin the discussion with the person of the Father[18] is all-important for Bonaventure because the First Person is the First Principle, or Cause, of all reality, both divine and created. Bonaventure utilizes an important philosophical principle that states that "the more primary a thing is, the more fecund it is, and it is [therefore] the principle of others."[19] As the eternal Origin, the Father communicates the divine substance (or divine being) eternally to the Son and to the Spirit. The Father is the divine person "who is not from another;" this distinguishing property is called *innascibilitas* (literally "not born" from another) and may be translated as "unbegottenness." The "Unbegotten One" is an accurate approximation in naming the First Person because it refers to the personal property that is unique to the Father and cannot be shared with the other two divine

---

[17] Théodore de Régnon, *Études de théologie positive sur la Sainte Trinité*, 3 vols. (Paris: Retoux, 1892-1889).

[18] John Scotus Eriugena (d. ca. 877) is said to have introduced the Greek trinitarian model to Western Christendom by way of his translations of the Pseudo-Dionysius (d. ca. 5th or early 6th century) which were available to Richard of St. Victor (d. 1173) and to Bonaventure's teacher, Alexander of Hales (d. 1245). De Régnon, vol.2, 240-42.

[19] I Sent., d.27, p.1, a.u., q.2, ad 3. *S. Bonaventurae opera omnia*, Volume I (Quaracchi: Collegium S. Bonaventurae, 1882), 470. All translations from the critical text of *The Sentences* are my own.

Bonaventure erroneously attributes this principle to Aristotle, but Ewert Cousins provides the correct source as the *Liber de causis,* prop.1 in *Bonaventure and the Coincidence of Opposites* (Chicago: Franciscan Herald Press, 1978), 53 and 295 n47.

Persons. For Bonaventure, the name of "Unbegotten One" offers pregnant negative and positive meanings. In the negative sense, "unbegotten" denotes an utter lack of a source, and thus establishes the Father as primary, truly the First Person. In the positive sense, the name connotes fecundity and establishes the Father as the sole Source of the divine essence; but the word "source" does not fully express the absolute fecundity in divinity. The Father is so perfectly, infinitely, and absolutely fecund, that Bonaventure employs the metaphor of *fontalis plenitudo* (fountain-fullness). It is the image of the moving, flowing, life-giving abundance of a spring; its lapping sounds convey a message of overflowing generosity. This paternal fecundity generates the Son and breathes forth the Spirit in eternity.

To speak about the "primacy of the Father" may grate on many people's ears, especially if it sounds as though subordinationism[20] were being introduced into the Trinity. This is because "primacy" is associated with being first in importance, rank, value, honor, and power; it implies leadership and preeminence. How are we to understand this, especially with regard to the Trinity which is a communion of equal persons-in-relation?

Let us start by saying that whatever we know about God the Father, we know through the Son and Spirit because God has revealed Godself in history. This statement suggests two points. One is that we should not divorce the Trinity from the history of salvation, which is made present today in the Church community, the Scriptures, and the sacraments. The second point is that we can know God only in history, only in time. God is eternal, and eternity is not "unending time," but the absence of time. There is no beginning and no end, no past and no future, but it has been said that there is an "ever-present." Therefore, there is no time sequence in eternity—the notion of "first, second, third," is repugnant to God. In this sense, then, the Father is not really "first" at all. No divine Person has primacy. But since we are all time-bound beings, we can speak about eternal things only in sequence and only by using verbs in their

---

[20] Subordinationism is a heresy concerning the Trinity that states that though the Son is divine he is not equal to the Father in being, attributes, and rank. This error was rejected at the Council of Nicea.

present, past, or future tenses. We do not have an "eternal verb tense." Therefore, the importance, status, and prominence that are often associated with "the first" have no reality in God.

Bonaventure also speaks of the Father as the "cause" or "origin" of the Son and Spirit, but this should not imply the literal beginning of the persons' existence: their existence is eternal. God was/is never without the divine Word and Spirit. Terms like "cause," "origin," and "source," are necessary because we have to begin somewhere to speak about the Trinity. There is no subordinationism within the Trinity. Perhaps our language itself reveals how "substantive," rather than relational, we are in our thinking and imagining.

Bonaventure understands divine primacy as eternal fecundity. He maintains as fact the philosophical axiom that "the more primary a thing is, the more fecund it is, and is therefore the origin of others."[21] Unquestionably, for Bonaventure, the Father's primacy means nothing other than this: Within God there is an unfathomable fecundity of mind and heart; an unfetterable, boundless expression of goodness, a fountain-fullness of self-transcending, Trinity-producing love who willingly overflows to fill the bottomless chasm between time and eternity so that we may be created, sanctified, and saved.

THE SELF-DIFFUSIVENESS OF THE GOOD

Another constitutive element for understanding Bonaventure's trinitarian theology is the philosophical principle that the nature of goodness is to be self-diffusive, which he derives from the Neoplatonic philosophy of the Pseudo-Dionysius.[22] The centrality of this principle cannot be over-estimated, because it

---

[21] I Sent., d.27, p.1, a.u., q.2, ad 3, 470.

[22] The Pseudo-Dionysus, *The Celestial Hierarchy*, IV.1 and *On the Divine Names*, IV.1, 20, in *Pseudo-Dionysius: The Complete Works*, The Classics of Western Spirituality Series (New York: Paulist Press, 1987).

is the grounds for the necessity of a tri-Personal God. It is also the basis for God's relation to the world.²³

In the first volume of the *Commentary on the Sentences*, Bonaventure discusses the question of why there ought to be a plurality of persons in God. He argues that supreme beatitude must necessarily abide in God. Supreme beatitude entails supreme goodness, perfect charity, complete simplicity, and primacy. A plurality of persons is essential for the fulfillment of these attributes, for "the possession of any good is not enjoyable for one who is without a companion."²⁴ We can see the importance of this principle of goodness as self-diffusive by examining Bonaventure's major work which formed generations of Franciscans, *The Soul's Journey into God*.

In the *Soul's Journey* Bonaventure leads the reader through six stages of mystical ascent (culminating in the seventh: the soul's passing over into God). The reader progresses from the contemplation of God in creation, to the divine image of the soul and finally, to the contemplation of God in Godself. The movement is from the exterior to the interior to the superior. Ever ascending, the movement within this highest stage is first, to contemplate the divine unity through its name which is Being, and then, to contemplate the Trinity in its name which is Goodness.²⁵

---

²³ The notion of self-diffusive goodness is not as developed in Bonaventure's earlier writings (*The Commentary on the Sentences, Disputed Questions on the Knowledge of Christ*, and *Disputed Questions on the Mystery of the Trinity*), as is the notion of the Father's fecund primacy or fountain-fullness.

²⁴ Seneca, *Epist.*, I, ad Lucilium, epist. 6, as quoted by Luc Mathieu, *La Trinité créatrice d'après saint Bonaventure* (Paris: Les Editions Franciscaines, 1992), 35: "La possession d'aucun bien n'est une jouissance pour celui qui est sans compagnon."

I Sent. d. 2, art.1, q. 2, 53: "si est ibi summa beatitudo; sed ubicumque est summa beatitudo, est summa bonitas, summa caritas et summa iucunditas. Sed si est summa bonitas, cum bonitatis sit summe se communicare, et hoc est maxime in producendo ex se aequalem et dando esse suum: ergo etc. Si summa caritas, cum caritas non sit amor privatus, sed ad alterum: ergo requirit pluralitatem. Item, si summa iucunditas, cum nullius boni sine socio sit iucunda possessio, ergo ad summam iucunditatem requiritur societas et ita pluralitas."

²⁵ Bonaventure, *The Soul's Journey into God*, chs. 5 and 6, respectively in *Itinerarium Mentis in Deum*, Works of Saint Bonaventure 2 (St. Bonaventure,

Bonaventure begins the meditation with God's own Self-naming disclosed to Moses in the Hebrew Scriptures: *Qui Est* or I Am Who Am (Ex 3:14). For Bonaventure, this is a proclamation of the unity of the divine substance.[26] Bonaventure receives the revealed name, and in the tradition of scholasticism, ushers the reader briefly through the attributes of divine Being: it is eternal, most simple, most powerful, infinite, immutable, perfect, most actual and hence pure act, and supremely one; and precisely because it is supremely one, it "is the universal principle of all multiplicity. By reason of this, it is the universal efficient, exemplary [formal], and final cause of all things."[27] Bonaventure presents the divine attributes in such a way as to have them flow logically from one into the other. Like his contemporary, Thomas Aquinas, Bonaventure describes B/being in the same Aristotelian categories of causality (i.e., efficient, formal, material, and final), of change (in terms of act and potency), and of reality (in terms of form and substance).

For Bonaventure, however, God's highest name is the Good,[28] for this is revealed in the New Testament in a verse in which Christ says, "No one is good but God alone" (Luke 18:19 and Matt 19:17). Since goodness and love are interchangeable, the quotation from the First Letter of John, "God is love" (1 John 4:8 and 16) is also relevant. In fact, it may be argued that the message that God is love and goodness is in keeping with the spirit of the New Testament as a whole. Bonaventure unites the fullest revelation of God in Christ with the Pseudo-Dionysian principle that the nature of the good is to be self-diffusive; and we can posit that there is a natural, fecund, and eternal emanation of divine life within the inner being of God.

The nature of goodness *per se* is such that it must go out of itself; it must be fecund and productive, ecstatic and self-communicative, generous and self-expressive. Goodness is dynam-

---

NY: Franciscan Institute Publications, 2002). Cf. I Sent., d.22, a.1, q.3, resp, 394-96.

[26] *The Soul's Journey*, 5:1. Cf. also Bonaventure, *The Collations on the Six Days*, 10:10 and 11:1 in The Works of Bonaventure V, trans. José de Vinck (Paterson, NJ: St. Anthony Guild Press, 1970).

[27] *The Soul's Journey*, 5:7.

[28] *The Soul's Journey*, 6:1-2.

ic: it must "act," it cannot merely "be." Therefore, the Father *must* be eternally and lovingly self-expressive by generating the Logos or Word. The Word must be a Person, not just an infinite number of abstract ideas, because rationality and love are the highest expression of God's Being, and because personhood is necessary for the perfection of love.[29] Certainly, we speak of goodness from our limited, relative, and imperfect experience of it. The nature of the good has been the object of concern, contemplation, and philosophical speculation for thousands of years, long before the Seraphic Doctor's academic sojourn in Paris. When Bonaventure lays claim to this Neoplatonic observation of the good's self-diffusive nature, he applies it analogously to an already well-developed Christian concept of God, which resonated with this philosophical principle.

In a remarkably concise and compact argument in the *Soul's Journey*, Bonaventure puts forth the quintessential trinitarian statement that sets him apart from any other theologian:

> See and take note that the highest good in an unqualified sense is that than which nothing better can be thought.[30] And this is of such a sort that it cannot be thought of as not existing, since it is absolutely better to exist than not to exist. And this is a good of such a sort that it cannot be thought of unless it is thought of as three and one. For "the good is said to be self-diffusive." The supreme good, therefore, is supremely self-diffusive. But the highest diffusion does not exist unless it is actual and intrinsic, substantial and personal, natural and voluntary, free and necessary, lacking nothing and perfect. In the supreme good there must be from eternity a production that is actual and consubstantial, and a hypostasis as noble as the producer, and this is the case in production by

---

[29] That personhood is necessary for the perfection of love is the central theme Bonaventure inherited from Richard of St. Victor. Cf. *The Trinity* in *Richard of St. Victor: The Twelve Patriarchs, The Mystical Ark, Book Three of the Trinity*, The Classics of Western Spirituality Series (New York: Paulist Press, 1979).

[30] Cf. Anselm's ontological argument in his *Proslogion* 1-5, in *St. Anselm: Basic Writings* (LaSalle, IL: Open Court Publishing, 1962), 15.

way of generation and spiration. This is understood to mean that what is of the eternal principle is of the eternal co-producer. In this way there can be both a beloved and a co-beloved, one generated and one spirated; that is, Father, and Son, and Holy Spirit. If this were not the case, it would not be the supreme good since it would not be supremely self-diffusive ...[31]

Because God is eternal, infinite, and perfect, God must, *by nature*, communicate Godself in an eternal, infinite, and perfect way, withholding no quality from the Son who is also called the Word and Image. This is the kenosis (self-emptying) of the Father. Because the Father communicates even the property of production (the ability to produce another), the Father and Son, together as one principle, spirate the Holy Spirit, who is also called Love and Bond. Because God is personal, divine self-expression produces an eternal communion of equal persons in loving relationship.

BONAVENTURE AND RICHARD OF ST. VICTOR

Bonaventure's Franciscan master at the University of Paris, Alexander of Hales, introduced him to the writings of Richard of St. Victor. Richard uses the analogy of human relationships to understand trinitarian relations. He understands the revelation of the Trinity in light of the human *experience* of relationships and on principles of logic. In the writings of both Richard and Bonaventure, goodness and love are convertible, for as Richard reasons, where there is full and perfect goodness, there is also love. Of all things that may be called "good," love is the best. Nothing is better than love, says Richard; nothing is more perfect.[32] Richard begins with the concept that God is supreme and perfect love, and in order to understand the nature of love better, he proceeds to discuss what has been learned of love from human relationships, namely that no one can be said to have

---

[31] *The Soul's Journey*, 6:2, 122-25.
[32] Richard of St. Victor, *The Trinity*, III:2.

love "on the basis of his own private love of himself."[33] Love by nature must be directed toward another. Therefore where a plurality of persons is lacking, love cannot exist. Love is by nature relational, and if God is love, then there must be a plurality of persons *in* God. God's love of Godself cannot properly be called love, for love must be directed toward another; nor is any creature capable of supreme love, for no creature is capable of the unimaginable heights and depths of this kind of intimacy.[34] Even if a human being were capable of such a loving relationship, this would make God *dependent* on a creature in order to be God, i.e., in order to express Godself as love. Thus, supreme, infinite divine love cannot be realized in the love of self nor in the love of a creature.

In order for love to be infinite, perfect, and supremely divine, it must be mutual. Thus, there must be a distinction of persons within the Godhead. The human experience of love makes it clear that *personhood* is necessary for the perfection of love. No other word, concept, analogy, or metaphor signifies the values necessary for love as the word "person" does, namely the capacity for mutuality, self-transcendence, dynamic self-communication, self-expression, rationality, self-donation and reception, generosity, sharing, community in diversity, intimacy, and fulfillment.[35]

The traditional model of the Trinity is such that the Father generates the Son from all eternity. The Son is the Logos—the Word or "Expressed Thought." The Father's Word must be the perfect, eternal, and infinite self-expression for it is of the Father's own substance. All that the Father knows and all that the Father is, is communicated in the generation of the Word. Since divinity is love and, therefore, *personal*, the Word must be a person. As a person, the Son loves the Father in return.

It may be argued that there is the perfect realization of the mutual love in the infinite self-donation of the Father's very

---

[33] Richard of St. Victor, *The Trinity*, III:2.
[34] Richard of St. Victor, *The Trinity*, III:2.
[35] These are the interpersonal values described throughout the article by Ewert Cousins, "A Theology of Interpersonal Relations," *Thought* 45 (1970): 56-81.

being to the Son, and in return, the Son loves the Father with the very same infinite love. And so, Richard asks why there is a third person in the Trinity and arrives at an astonishing insight:

> In true charity, it seems excellent to wish another to be loved as one's self. Certainly in mutual and very fervent love nothing is rarer or more magnificent than to *wish that another be loved equally* by the one whom you love supremely and by whom you are supremely loved. *And so the proof of perfected charity is a willing sharing of the love that has been shown to you.*... So a person proves that he is not perfect in charity if he cannot yet take pleasure in sharing his excellent joy.... Therefore it is necessary that each of those loved supremely and loving supremely should search with equal desire for someone who would be mutually loved with equal concord...[36]

Perfect realization of supreme love, then, is *not* realized in the mutual love of two persons; there is still the slightest suggestion of selfishness. It is clear that two persons are necessary for the kind of relationship that is truly loving, that is, a relationship in which there is full and mutual self-transcendence. Richard maintains that the perfection of love demands three persons. Richard bases this assertion not on logic, but on the highest human experience: to truly love another is the highest good and it is self-transcendence. To have that love returned is mutually fulfilling, but incomplete; for what could be more perfect, what could be the very height of self-transcendence, than to go beyond this closed binary and to desire this very experience of mutual love for a third person? Supreme love is realized in the love of two shared generously with a third. This is self-transcending love, which is fulfilled in the mutual love of three persons, that is, in a perfect community in diversity. Note the echoes of Richard's "interpersonal Trinity" in Bonaventure's final and mature work, *The Collations*:

---

[36] Richard, *The Trinity*, III.11 (emphasis added).

It occurs by necessity that wherever happiness is, love be there also, and consequently, love in the highest degree. Now love is reflexive, unitive, charitable. Unitive love, which is the love of another, is better than reflexive love, which is the love of self; but charitable love is even better than either of these, for it has a beloved and a co-beloved; therefore, this is the love which abides in divinity. With this love, therefore, does the Father love the Son in infinite ardor. Also, here is a love which is freely given, owed, and mutual. Here is a pure, full, and perfect love that flows out and overflows in the Son, so that it flows back in the Holy Spirit.[37]

Even though the Son and Spirit proceed from the Unbegotten Father as their Source, the three must be equal for love to be mutually fulfilling. The processions are eternal, thus, there can be no time sequence—no first, second, or third. The self-donation of the Father's very being is infinite and lacking nothing; only then can there be an eternally *dynamic* circle of infinite self-donation and infinite reception. Love, the highest expression of the Good, necessitates a plurality of persons in God, but the mutual love between Father and Son is not enough. A greater love can be conceived: that this love overflows in abundance, generosity, and perfect freedom to a third person.[38] The Holy Spirit proceeds from the mutual love of Father and Son and *is* their Love. The highest good is not actualized unless it produces consubstantial and equal Persons.

At the risk of sounding rationalistic, Bonaventure puts forth the "necessary reasons" for the Trinity. He draws from Aristotle's principle that there are only two modes of production: natural and free.[39] The Son is necessarily generated by the self-diffusive nature and is the Word of the divine intellect, while the Spirit is freely spirated in liberality and is the Love from the divine will.

---

[37] Bonaventure, *The Collations on the Six Days*, 11:12.

[38] I Sent., d.10, a.1, q.1, fund. 1, 195.

[39] Bonaventure, *The Breviloquium*, I:3.2 in *Breviloquium*, trans. and ed. Dominic V. Monti, O.F.M., Works of Saint Bonaventure 9 (St. Bonaventure, NY: Franciscan Institute Publications, 2005).

Both kinds of productions are fulfilled.⁴⁰ As Zachary Hayes explains it, if all the *possible* ways in which the good can communicate itself were not fully expressed in the two emanations of the divine intellect and will, then the production would not be perfect; but there can be no imperfection in God. On the other hand, if all the possible ways of communication *are* expressed in the two emanations, then any other would be superfluous; but this too would be an imperfection in God. Thus, there must be two and only two emanations in God.⁴¹

Finally, another line of argument is drawn from the five notions (innascibility, paternity, filiation, active spiration, and passive spiration): the Father is from no other but produces only. The Spirit does not produce, but is receptive only; the Son is both productive and receptive.⁴² Thus, all the possibilities have been exhausted,⁴³ and the Son is established as the *Persona Media* or the Central Person within the Trinity.⁴⁴

BONAVENTURE AND GREEK PATRISTIC TRINITARIAN THEOLOGY

Bonaventure's trinitarian theology is often characterized as Cappadocian, or Greek patristic, and this is true insofar as he begins his expositions with the distinctiveness of the divine persons, rather than with the unifying divine substance. The Cappadocian Fathers embraced the term "monarchy of the Father" (or the *monarchia* of the Father). It means that the Father is unbegotten and does not come from another, and is thereby the sole and unifying Principle of the Trinity. "*Mone arche*" in Greek means "one principle" or "one source." Unfortunately, the term can also be understood as "one rule," but that is not what the Cappadocians meant; they were interested in establishing the

---

⁴⁰ Bonaventure, *Disputed Questions on the Mystery of the Trinity*, IV.a.2, ad 1, Works of Saint Bonaventure 3, trans. Zachary Hayes, ed. George Marcil (St. Bonaventure, NY: The Franciscan Institute, 1979).

⁴¹ Hayes, "Introduction," in *Mystery of the Trinity*, 90.

⁴² Bonaventure, *Mystery of the Trinity*, 53.

⁴³ I Sent., d.2, a.u., q.4, resp., 57-58. Also *The Soul's Journey*, 6:2.

⁴⁴ I Sent., d.27, p.2, a.u., q.2, resp., 485-86. Also *The Collations*, 1:14.

unity of the Trinity in the Person of the Father, and not in subordinating the Son and Spirit.

It is also true that Bonaventure's trinitarian theology is Cappadocian insofar as he does not expound at any significant length about the nature of God apart from the doctrine of the Trinity. We do not find, for example, in any of Bonaventure's writings, a paradigm similar to Thomas Aquinas who separated the discussion on the doctrine of God into two treatises: *De Deo uno* and *De Deo trino*, i.e., "On the One God" and "On the Triune God." This separation was conducive to the study of God "as God is in Godself," which, as Karl Rahner laments, "has prevailed ever since" in the West so that "… the Trinity locks itself in even more splendid isolation."[45] In eschewing the Augustinian-Thomistic trinitarian approach, Bonaventure avoids many of the pitfalls of a trinitarian model which is self-contained and isolated.[46] Sadly, this Franciscan tradition did not become the dominant tradition in theology, and until recently was little known.

In Bonaventure's theology God is perfect, infinite, eternal, and absolute goodness. Since the good is by nature self-diffusive, God by nature *must* diffuse Godself in a perfect, infinite, eternal, and absolute way. Just as Thomas held that God's essence is existence itself,[47] Bonaventure holds that God's essence is goodness itself. Therefore, God's essential goodness is the wellspring for the Second Person who is Son, Word, and Image. "Father" is a relational term, which indicates that one person comes forth from another. The Father begets the Son because God is love;[48] and interpersonal relationship is necessary for the perfection of love. God generates the *Logos* because God must

---

[45] Karl Rahner, *The Trinity* (New York: Herder and Herder, 1970), 16-17.

[46] Catherine Mowry LaCugna, *God For Us: The Trinity and Christian Life* (San Francisco: Harper, 1991), 143-49.

[47] Thomas Aquinas, *Summa Theologicae* Ia, q.3, a.4 concl. in *The Basic Writings of Saint Thomas Aquinas* I, ed. Anton Pegis (New York: Random House, 1945). Bonaventure does not hold that we can literally know God's essence, for it is by nature incomprehensible to finite beings. We are speaking analogically. Thomas also holds that we cannot know *what* God is, but only *that* God is: *Summa* Ia q.2. and q.3, a.4, obj. 2.

[48] Love is the highest good, and love and goodness are convertible.

express the divine ideas, and the Word is the fullest expression of Godself. God produces the *Image* because the Image reflects all that the Father infinitely is, and returns the Father's love as only an infinite person can. This reciprocated love is the Holy Spirit acting as the gift and the bond between them.

The Father is the highly dynamic Source of the twofold diffusion, one within Godself which is the procession of equal persons in the unity of nature, and the other is outside of God which is the creation of the universe that participates in goodness in a limited, imperfect way.[49] This is a highly fecund, ecstatic, and dynamic understanding of God. In generating the Son, the Father withholds nothing in the perfect kenosis of Godself into the Son. The Son is even given the property of production, and thus, the Father and the Son, together as one principle, spirate the Holy Spirit. This is an eternal communion of total self-giving and self-receiving of divine life and being, the paradigm of love. It is an ecstatic divine dance, eternally initiated by the Father.

If love is such that it withholds absolutely nothing, not even the very property of production, then the Father, the Son, and the Spirit are perfectly, infinitely, eternally, and absolutely equal. If the Son is not perfectly equal to the Father, and the Spirit as well, then the Father's self-diffusion, self-expression, or self-donation is not perfect, and God's nature remains unfulfilled. The Father is the wellspring of divine generosity which may be defined as the capacity and the desire to communicate what one has; and what is eternally communicated to the Son and Spirit is the Father's own infinite Being.

One of the most unique characteristics of Bonaventure's trinitarian theology is that he unites the principle of the Father's primordial fecundity and the principle of the divine nature as self-diffusive goodness. The application of these principles to trinitarian speculation produces *necessity* in God. God *must* be a plurality of persons. The Father *must*, by nature, generate the Son. Even though Bonaventure is (correctly) likened to the Greek patristic writers, especially the Cappadocians, this no-

---

[49] I Sent., d.19, p.1, a.1, q.2, ad 3, 345.

tion of "necessary emanation" resulting from the self-diffusive goodness, as Bonaventure applies it to trinitarian doctrine, is quite unique to him alone. While the theme of the unbegottenness of the Father is prevalent in the Cappadocian writings,[50] the notion that God must necessarily be a plurality of divine persons, or that the Father *must* beget the Son, is not found. Gregory Nazianzen, for example, in his battles against the heresy of Eunomious, advises against even posing the question of *how* or *why* the Son is generated.[51]

BONAVENTURE AND PROCESS THEOLOGY

The concept of God in process theology makes God dependent on the universe in order for God to express Godself in creation.[52] If God is to be understood as dynamic and productive in this metaphysical system of process philosophy, then the universe is necessary for divine self-fulfillment. The universe would have to be eternal in order to be coextensive with God. Creation could never be an act of divine freedom and love, but a necessary emanation so that divine creativity may be realized. In Bonaventure's system the locus for the realization of divine expression or productivity is within the inner life of the Godhead itself. Thus, the Son, not the universe, is the necessary emanation, and a most fitting one, for the infinite nature of God is fulfilled infinitely within the Trinity and without making God dependent on creation. God's nature is also realized most personally in the Son who is the perfect image of the Father, and who can thereby reciprocate in love. Bonaventure's theology of the Trinity makes creation an utterly free act and the creature

---

[50] For a discussion on "the unbegottenness of the Father," in the Cappadocians, see LaCugna, *God For Us*, 60-68.

[51] Gregory Nazianzen, *Orations*, XXIX.8 (On the Son), in *A Select Library of Nicene and Post-Nicene Fathers* VII, ed. Philip Schaff and Henry Wace (Grand Rapids: Eerdmans, 1983).

[52] Cf. Alfred North Whitehead, *Process and Reality* (New York: MacMillan, 1929), 515-33; Charles Hartshorne, *Man's Vision of God and the Logic of Theism* (Chicago: Wellet, Clark, 1941). For a discussion of Bonaventure and process philosophy, see Cousins, *Bonaventure and the Coincidence of Opposites*, 239-47.

a unique expression of God's totally free generosity and goodness.

Bonaventure's Doctrine of Exemplarity

Although God is perfectly fulfilled in the infinite self-expression of the Son within the Trinity, God freely chooses to create the universe. All creation is an expression of God's goodness. Just as a work of art is an expression of the artist, God expresses Godself as Trinity in the universe. Bonaventure calls this doctrine "exemplarity," and it is at the heart of his metaphysics. For Bonaventure, the metaphysician does not engage in vain, self-serving curiosity when trying to understand the nature of reality,[53] but ponders individual, created realities in such a way as to rise to the universal Uncreated Reality of Being itself. Even so, this ascent does not attain to the reality of the Father, Son, and Holy Spirit, unless one contemplates, in the light of revelation, this notion of Being itself as the *exemplary* cause of all created things. The true metaphysician is the one who rises to the Trinity, not by philosophy alone, but through an understanding of exemplarity.[54] Exemplarity is at the heart of Bonaventure's overall view of reality as we know it here and now: "This is our whole metaphysics: emanation, exemplarity, consummation.... And thus you will be a true metaphysician."[55]

There are, then, three distinct movements to this decidedly dynamic view of reality. The first is emanation—the voluntary *exitus* or flowing out of creation when God spoke into what is not God. The next is exemplarity—encountering God in a trinitarian self-expression in every created existent (including human beings); and this encounter leads us up a ladder in an ascent back to the Creator. Bonaventure calls the return to our Source the "reduction" (from *re-ducere*—"to lead back"). We arrive at the third movement, consummation, or union with God.

---

[53] *The Collations*, 1:8.
[54] *The Collations*, 1:13.
[55] *The Collations*, 1:17.

Exemplarity refers to the manifestation of the Trinity in the universe, and it is the concept that expresses God's closeness to creation. By the contemplation of exemplarity we are led to the First Cause—the concern of every metaphysician—who is God the Father, and to the Eternal Exemplar who is God the Son and through whom the Father created the universe, and to the Sanctifier who is God the Holy Spirit in whom we are sustained. The connection between the created and the uncreated, in this metaphysical system, is the Son and Exemplar. The Son is the Logos[56] or Word of the Father. That is to say, the Word is the "Exemplar" of all that God infinitely is and all that God can lovingly do. The Exemplar is the pre-existent expression of the infinite *rationes necessariae*,[57] which are more easily understood as the Platonic eternal forms, now the divine ideas in the mind of God. The *rationes necessariae* are the eternal forms of everything ever created and ever creat*able*. Thus, the Son is the Word or the Exemplar, "through Whom all things were made" (John 1:3), as the Creed professes.

All created beings, then, disclose the triune God as their efficient, formal (exemplary), and final Cause. This is to say that all things proclaim God as their source and as their ultimate aim or purpose. With regard to their formal cause, creatures exemplify God's power (as their Creator *ex nihilo*), wisdom (as their Logos or "reasoned ordering"), and goodness (as their sanctifier and final end).[58] Every existent refers to God in its triple causality. Bonaventure sees traces of the Trinity in every creature, and therefore calls them "vestiges" (literally, "footprints" or "imprints") of the Trinity.[59] A vestige reflects God's power, wis-

---

[56] Any one of the many meanings of the Greek word "logos" is suitable for the Second Person, e.g., word, thought (a "word" is an "expressed thought") reason, understanding, speech, and order. "Logos" is connected with the intellectual faculty.

[57] *Rationes necesssariae, rationes aeternae*, divine ideas, necessary ideas, eternal ideas, eternal reasons, eternal art, and exemplar all refer to the Logos and may be used interchangeably.

[58] Cf. *The Soul's Journey*, 1:10 and 1:14; *Mystery of the Trinity*, IV.1, 12.

[59] *The Soul's Journey*, esp. 1:10 and 1:14, and ch. 2.

dom, and goodness as correlated to the Father, Son, and Spirit, respectively.[60]

Human beings are vestiges, but they are more worthily called "images" of God, for they reflect the Trinity in the capacity for, and function of, memory, intellect, and will.[61] The triadic human faculties (which are constitutive of our humanity) are correlated to the Persons of the Father, the Son, and the Holy Spirit, respectively.[62] Those human beings who, by grace and free will, draw closer to God go from being images of God to being "similitudes," i.e., "God conformed."[63]

The created order can lead people to God; that is, if they choose to look beyond the creatures themselves toward the Creator. This notion is Bonaventure's rational articulation of the Franciscan spiritual *experience*: "In beautiful things he [Francis] contuited Beauty itself and through the footprints impressed in things he followed his Beloved everywhere, out of them all making for himself a ladder through which he could climb up to lay hold of him who is utterly desirable."[64] Bonaventure posits a hierarchy of being in the universe, using the metaphor of the ladder of creation. In contemplating the "rungs" of creatures (including ourselves), in the light of faith, human beings ascend to their Creator.[65] This is the purpose of exemplarity, which is undoubtedly the result of mystical insight. Yet, exemplarity is not without its philosophical logic. The well-accepted philosophical principle that "every effect is the sign of its cause" is at

---

[60] *The Soul's Journey*, 2:14.

[61] *The Soul's Journey*, esp. 3:1 and 3:5, and ch.4. Also *Mystery of the Trinity*, I:2, con.

[62] Bonaventure inherited the "psychological trinity" from Augustine. Cf. Augustine, *On the Trinity*, Bk. X, The Fathers of the Church Series 45 (Washington: CUA Press, 1963), 291-313.

[63] *Breviloquium*, II.12:1.

[64] Bonaventure, *The Major Legend of Saint Francis* (*The Life of Blessed Francis*), 9.1 in *Francis of Assisi: Early Documents*, Vol. II: *The Founder*, ed. Regis J. Armstrong, J.A. Wayne Hellman,, and William J. Short (Hyde Park, NY: New City Press, 2000). The word "contuited" is a translation of *contuebatur*, a verb form of the Latin word *contuitus*, which can be translated as "concomitant insight"; see FAED 2, 532 n.d and 596 n.a. "Contuition" is the indirect apprehension of higher reality.

[65] *The Soul's Journey*, 1:2.

work here (also stated as "the cause is in the effect"). Arguments from causality and from design can be made to undergird the legitimacy of exemplarity as a philosophical system. Exemplarity represents a way of dealing with enduring questions: What is our place and purpose in the universe? Who are we and what are we to do?

Exemplarity tells us: 1) that we are images of the triune God in our capacity for memory, intellect, and will; 2) that because we are trinitarian images of God, human beings are of infinite worth and dignity; 3) that we enter the metaphysical circle as its apex among countless vestiges in creation; 4) that we can use our memory, intellect, and will to know and to love God in and through created things; and 5) that we return to the Creator through Christ who is the Father's Exemplar, and in the Spirit who is our strength. Bonaventure sums up the preceding discussion about the emanations within God and outside of God as exemplarity in the concluding sentences of his *Disputed Questions on the Mystery of the Trinity*:

> For, since the Father brings forth the Son, and through the Son, and together with the Son brings forth the Holy Spirit, God the Father through the Son and with the Holy Spirit is the principle of everything created; for if he did not produce them eternally, he could not produce anything in time; and therefore he is rightly called the "Font of Life."... Therefore it follows that eternal life consists in this alone, that the rational spirit, which emanates from the most blessed Trinity and is a likeness of the Trinity, should return after the manner of a certain intelligible circle through its memory, intelligence, and will to the most blessed Trinity by God-conforming glory.[66]

The role of the Second Person of the Trinity is clearly central to both intra-divine life and extra-divine reality. Bonaventure's trinitarianism, for all its philosophical speculation, is not skewed away from the *history* of salvation nor from the faith

---

[66] *Mystery of the Trinity*, VIII, ad ob. 7, 266.

experience of the Church. What keeps Bonaventure's Trinity grounded in the economy of salvation is a Franciscan *Christocentricity*. As we shall see when we see the foundations of Bonaventure's thought in Francis's spiritual experience, Franciscan spirituality is not overly concerned with speculation about the eternal ideas in the mind of God. This spirituality is known for its devotion to the humanity of Christ. It is also known for its tradition of imitating the historical Jesus of Nazareth, especially in his virtues of poverty, humility, and love; and for its preaching of Christ's redemptive death and resurrection as the way to salvation. The devotion to the humanity of Christ may be seen in the Franciscan tradition's emphasis on the defining parameters of human life: birth and death. Francis has been credited with starting the enduring tradition of the Christmas crèche; and his spirituality is focused on the Passion, so much so that the stigmata was the confirmation of his imitation of Christ. His experiential spirituality gives a large place to the person's relationship with the Father, the Son, and the Spirit. Bonaventure's spiritual theology in *The Soul's Journey* systematizes this path of the following of Christ; his Trinitarian theology grounds it in its highest speculative dimensions.

THE SON

According to Bonaventure, God's infinite fecundity is infinitely realized in mutual *relationality* because the natural and eternal emanation of the Father's overflowing, loving goodness is a *Person*. The title "Son" connotes both origin and a personal relationship.

If God is supreme goodness—that than which no greater goodness can be thought—then the greatest Self-diffusion must be a divine person who is perfectly equal to the producer and one in being; otherwise God would not be supreme Goodness.[67] From all eternity the Father generates the Son, and withholds nothing in this divine kenosis or self-emptying. Therefore, the

---

[67] *The Soul's Journey*, 6:3. Also I Sent., d.2, a.1, q.2, fund. 1, 53.

Father and the Son, as well as the Holy Spirit, are by nature and necessity perfectly equal persons. The Father withholds nothing from the Son so that all that the Father is—*whatever* the Father is[68]—the Son is also, and thus they are one. The Son, as the true image, is all the goodness that the Father is, and so loves the Father in return from all eternity. This love is also a person, the Holy Spirit, their bond and mutual gift. This is a perfect love who breathes forth in absolute liberality. Persons worthy and capable of this divine and mutual love must be equal to the Father. If the Son and Spirit are not absolutely all that the Father is, then the begetting would be defective; the production, deficient; and the giving, mean and miserly.

The Greek trinitarian tradition which Bonaventure adopts as his own is defined as *orthodox* on the very basis of the Son's and the Spirit's perfect equality to the Father. Over the centuries, half the ink spilled in the Christological controversies was in defense of the divinity of the Son who is, as Gregory of Nazianzus upholds, "True God and equal to the Father."[69]

THE SON AS IMAGE AND WORD

Thus far, the discussion on the Son has centered on Bonaventure's understanding of the nature of relationality and of the essential equality of the three persons. If the Son is all that the Father is, then the Son is the perfect image of the Father. What might this mean? For Bonaventure the term "image" designates the Son's "expressed likeness" to the Father.[70] This "likeness" is not a mere reflection, but the eternal, *perfect*, and *substantial* expression of the Father (any expression *in* God must be of the highest order). There can be only one designated as the image, because there is only one perfect *expression* of the Father; any other would be either superfluous or would mean that the Son,

---

[68] Only the Father's unbegottenness cannot be communicated or shared; this property—being the Source of divine life—distinguishes the Father.

[69] Gregory of Nazianzus, *Orations*, XXIX.17 (Third Oration—On the Son), NPNF.

[70] *Breviloquium*, I.3:8.

as the image, lacked some quality, and therefore it would not be the perfect expression. Only the Son, and not the Spirit, is image of the Father because the Son proceeds from one person, while the Spirit proceeds from both Father and Son as one Principle. The Spirit expresses both equally but neither fully. Since the Son is the image of the Father, this likeness to the Father is substantial and perfect enough to produce the Spirit, but not enough to blur the distinction of the persons,[71] for the Father remains the one who is Unbegotten.

In the *Breviloquium* Bonaventure succinctly sums up the three titles of the Second Person as "Image, Word, and Son:" this person is named Image as expressed likeness, Word as expressing likeness, and Son as personal likeness.[72] Each title is meant to convey an unmistakable equality and a close unity with the Father: the Image in the order of form *(conformem)*, Word in the order of intellect *(intellectualem),* and Son in the order of nature *(connaturalem).*[73] For Bonaventure the titles imply and telescope into each other, for he says, regarding the Second Person, *"because* he is the Son, properly speaking, he is also the Image; and precisely *as* Son and Image, he is also Word."[74] Bonaventure's understanding of the Second Person is consonant with the Scriptural verse from Colossians that says,

> He [Christ] is the image of the invisible God, the firstborn of creation; for in him all things were created, in heaven and on earth, visible and invisible … all things were created through him and for him. He is before all things, and in him all things hold together (Col 1:15-17).

This passage is scripturally fundamental to naming the Son as Image, of course, but the designation of the Word, as the Eternal Exemplar "through whom all things were created," is also grounded in this passage (as well as in John 1:1-3). It may

---

[71] I Sent., d.31, p.2, a.1, q.2, conclu., 535-36.
[72] *Breviloquium*, I.3:8.
[73] *Breviloquium*, I.3:8.
[74] I Sent., d.31, p.2, a.1, q.2, conclu., 535-36.

be characterized as a "functional" Christology, but it alludes to the preexistence of the Image and, thus it unites the Son's role in the Trinity and in creation. Finally, it is reminiscent of Christ the center, "who holds all things together." However, "Word" is a multi-valent metaphor; it indicates intellect, the divine ideas, self-expression, the Exemplar or pattern for all existents, the Word made flesh, revelation, etc.

There are two kinds of emanations in God: one intellectual and one volitional, and these exhaust all the possible modes of expression proper to personhood (i.e., knowing and loving). From all eternity the Son proceeds forth as the Logos, God's Word from the divine intellect; and the Holy Spirit is breathed forth as God's Love from the divine will. In this Word all divine reality is eternally communicated within Godself: i.e., God's ideas (*rationes necessariae*), God's love, God's very Being. As the perfect expression of God's self-diffusive goodness, the Word is all that God is and all that God can do.

Bonaventure prefers the designation of Word, because, in contrast to "Son" and "Image," "Word" points to a relation with both the Father and creation.[75] Every theologian's Christology calls Christ "the Word," but in Bonaventure's trinitarian theology, with its exemplaristic cast, the Word as the expressing exemplar "holds together" the speculation about the inner life of the Trinity *and* the revelation of the Trinity made known in salvation history. Although Bonaventure speculates and reasons at great length about the intra-divine personal relations, origins, and properties, his Trinity is never completely divorced from the doctrines of creation, the Incarnation, the economy of salvation, nor from theological anthropology. In an exemplaristic universe, as *The Soul's Journey* argues, Bonaventure truly sees, in the light of faith, traces (vestiges) of the Trinity in each creature[76] and he truly encounters the triune God in his own soul, the divine image.[77] Humans enter the metaphysical circle of *exitus* and *reductio*, and are offered the opportunity to seek God's

---

[75] I Sent., d.31, p.2, a.1, q.2, conclu., 535-36. Cf. Hayes, *Mystery of the Trinity*, 51.
[76] *The Soul's Journey*, chs. 1 and 2.
[77] *The Soul's Journey*, chs. 3 and 4.

power, wisdom, and goodness[78] (appropriated to the Father, Son, and Spirit) in all creation. Bearing not only a trace of the Trinity, but its image (however imperfect) in our memory, intellect, and will, we *use* our memory, intellect, and will, to contemplate the trinitarian vestiges and images. Through sense knowledge we abstract the ideas or forms of created existents into our minds, receive them within us, so to speak, and then take them with us for they have served their purpose.[79] The material world, that which Bonaventure calls the macrocosm, enters the soul, (the microcosm) through the five senses on the journey to God in the *reductio*.[80] This journey would seem inordinately abstract and even esoteric, if it were not grounded in the historical Christ.[81] Franciscan tradition and spirituality[82] grounds Bonaventure's metaphysics in the historical Jesus of Nazareth, in the devotion to his humanity, in an authentic imitation of his life,[83] and in his salvific death and resurrection.

CHRISTOCENTRICITY

In Bonaventure's overall theology the Word is the expressed thought of the divine mind, the *rationes necessariae* (or divine ideas) of everything ever created and creat*able*. The Word is the Second Person of the Trinity and the medium through whom the cosmos was created. The Word is also the one who truly assumed a human body and soul, the babe in Mary's arms dependent on her care, Jesus who lived a fully—though sinless—human life; Jesus who truly suffered and died, but rose to new life. Because Jesus is the eternal and timeless Word immanent in

---

[78] *The Soul's Journey*, 1:14.
[79] *The Soul's Journey*, 2:11.
[80] *The Soul's Journey*, 2:2.
[81] While Jesus of Nazareth is fully human, he is also the Word, the embodiment of *rationes necessariae*.
[82] Although Bonaventure is a scholastic of the thirteenth century, the split between spiritual experience and rational consciousness has not *fully* occurred in his theology, as it has in later Western/Latin theology.
[83] For a discussion on Franciscan spirituality and the imitation of Christ, see Zachary Hayes, *The Hidden Center: Spirituality and Speculative Christology in St. Bonaventure* (St. Bonaventure, NY: Franciscan Institute, 2000), 25-52.

history, his death and resurrection are redemptive for all people at all times. Christ is the center of all history, of all time, and of all humanity. As the Word is the medium of creation, so also the Word made flesh is the means of salvation. He is the way back to God in the stages of our spiritual ascent of purgation, illumination, and perfection/union.[84] He enlightens, purifies, and unites us in the very life of God; the Word became human so that we may become divine. The dynamic movement is "from the Father and to the Father"[85] within the inner life of the Trinity and within the history of salvation.

Because Bonaventure has a Cappadocian understanding of the Trinity *within* an exemplaristic universe, the Word inextricably binds the Trinity to creation and to creation's consummation. The activity of the Trinity is evident in the history of salvation; and its presence may be found in the hearts of human beings everywhere and at all times.

"Christocentricity" is the traditional term that refers to the second person who is the *persona media*[86] or the central person *within* the Trinity, but who is also the person *between* the Trinity and creation ("through whom all things were made"). As the Incarnate One, the second person is the *center* of creation, history, and the Christian life.[87] "Christocentricity," then, would be an accurate term when it refers to the Incarnate Word's earthly mission and metaphysical significance, but it would be technically misleading to project the human (and male) Christ into the eternal Trinity. Perhaps, "Logoscentricity" would be a slightly more precise term because "Logos" is used to designate both the preexisting Second Person of the Trinity and the historical

---

[84] *The Soul's Journey*, 1:8 and 4:4.

[85] LaCugna, *God For Us*, 223.

[86] There is nothing intrinsically or existentially male about the preexisting second person or the *persona media,* and this fact extends, of course, to the titles of Word (Logos), Image, Wisdom, or even to the *preexisting* "Son." However, "Son" is a male metaphor, rather than a gender-neutral metaphor; it does evoke a male image in a way that the other metaphors do not. Nevertheless, the Son is no more male than God is, and "Son" is an essential relational term, not a proper name.

[87] In the First Collation (1:11-39) of *The Collations*, Bonaventure intends to show that all the treasures of God's wisdom and knowledge are hidden in Christ, and that he is the center of all understanding.

Jesus of Nazareth who is the Word Incarnate. Nevertheless, in the interest of a common and consistent terminology, "Christocentricity" is used in this work to refer to the Second Person both in the immanent Trinity and in the Incarnation.

Early in his works, Bonaventure posits the Son as the central person in the life of the Trinity and he develops this theme of Christocentricity throughout his writings until his last work, *The Collations on the Six Days*. Within the Trinity the Son is the dynamic center between the Father and the Spirit, and so, is the middle person between the Father who only produces and the Spirit who only is produced. The Son both is produced and produces, both receives and gives divine life.[88] As Zachary Hayes explains it, this is

> ... the order of divine life; and in this is grounded the fact that all which flows from God in the form of creation has a beginning, a middle, and an end. The movement of emanation in creation and in grace is grounded in this metaphysical understanding of the divinity ... The eternal Son who is the center of the Trinity, and who mediates all the divine works of creation and illumination, in becoming incarnate assumes his place as the center of the created universe and its history. Thus, theology, Christology, anthropology, creation, illumination, revelation are brought together tightly around the one universal center of meaning, hidden to human eyes by reason of sin and revealed in the history of the suffering, incarnate Word.[89]

The *persona media* of the Trinity becomes the axis of history and the center of creation, for all reality centers in him: the divine reality as Word, the material reality of his flesh, and the spiritual reality of his soul.

The Franciscan emphasis on Christ the Center is faithful to the history of salvation in which the Father creates, redeems, sanctifies, and saves through the Son and in the power of the

---

[88] I Sent., d.2, a.u., q.4, conclu., 57-58. *The Soul's Journey*, 6:2.
[89] Hayes, *The Hidden Center*, 62.

Spirit. Christocentricity allows us to start any kind of theology, including trinitarian theology *from the center* (i.e., with Christ). In the *First Collation*, Bonaventure states that, when giving a sermon, the prudent know "they ought to begin from the center, who is Christ, for if the center is neglected, nothing is obtained."[90] Thus, when we recount God's salvific activity in history, it is natural to begin with Christ the center because that is how God the Father *comes to us*—through Christ and in the Spirit. In contrast, when we organize our knowledge about God derived from the account of God's salvific activity, and then speculate about the implications of our knowledge, we begin with the Father.

"In Whom All Things Hold Together" (Col 1:17)

The Son as the *persona media* "holds together" what may be called polar opposites in the Trinity. Between the Father, who produces but is not produced, and the Spirit, who is produced but does not produce, there is the Son, who is produced and also produces.[91] In a similar manner, the Father is only active and giving, while the Spirit is only passive and receptive, but the Son is passive and receptive and also active and giving. All the possibilities are exhausted in this configuration, and the Son is at the center of them all, "holding them together" as the coexistence of complementary opposites. The complementary opposites are united and reconciled, but not merged; the differences are intensified. The Word can be imagined as the one who "holds together" two interlocking circles: as the *persona media* of the Trinity, the Word unites the three divine Persons in a circular dance of dynamic and eternal self-transcending love. As Christ, the Word unites all extra-divine realities in the metaphysical circle (of emanation, exemplarity, and consummation). In him time and space, matter and form, the physical and the spiritual are "held together." The Word is *through* whom all these realities came into being; *of* whom all things exemplify (as their Exem-

---

[90] *The Collations*, 1:1.
[91] I Sent., d.2, a.u. q.4, concl., 57-58. *The Soul's Journey*, 6:3.

plar); and *by* whom all things return. (The Word is also *through* whom we are saved, and *for* whom all exist and will ever exist.) In Christ *all* realities are "held together": the divine reality in his being the Son and Word, the material reality in his human body, and the spiritual reality in his human soul.

The Holy Spirit

Just as the Son proceeds as the Word, the expression of God's mind, so the Spirit proceeds as Love,[92] the expression of God's will. Therefore in the two divine processions, all expressions proper to personhood are realized, one intellectual and one volitional (as intellect and free will, the capacity to know and to love constitute us as human persons). Any other emanation would be superfluous and would mar divine perfection.

The Pseudo-Dionysian principle of the good is joined with the Victorine analysis of human love in Bonaventure's understanding of the Person of the Holy Spirit. Even mutually fulfilling love is not perfect unless it transcends the possible *égoisme a deux* and truly desires this same perfectly mutual love for another,[93] so that, as Bonaventure says in the *Soul's Journey*, there may be a beloved and a co-beloved (*Dilectus et Condilectus*).[94] It is wise and highly insightful to observe that "mutual love is more perfect than self-love, and a mutually shared love is better than one that is not shared, because a love of that kind, namely unshared love, is considered to smack of selfish desire."[95]

The Spirit is called Love, Bond, and Gift.[96] The Holy Spirit may be understood as divine love in three related ways: first, the Spirit is love insofar as the Spirit is God who is essentially love. Second, the Spirit is also the love who proceeds from the divine will. Lastly, the love with which the Father loves the Son, and with which the Son loves the Father, is also a person, name-

---

[92] I Sent., d.6, a.u., q.3, conclu., 129-30.
[93] Cf. Richard of St. Victor, *The Trinity*, III:15.
[94] *The Soul's Journey*, 6:2, 123-25. Also I Sent., d.10, a.1, q.1, fund.1, 194-95.
[95] I Sent., d.10, a.1, q.1, fund.1, 194-95.
[96] *Breviloquium*, I.3:9.

ly the Holy Spirit.⁹⁷ In this sense the Third Person unites Father and Son, and so, is called their Bond of Love. In the *Breviloquium*, Bonaventure writes that it is the unique and personal property of the Holy Spirit to be "Gift," the One Given *par excellence* through the divine will of the Father and the Son.⁹⁸ It is the distinguishing property of the Third Person to be produced, and not to produce, to come forth from the *fontalis plenitudo* or fountain-fullness of the infinitely free and absolutely good divine will. The Holy Spirit, therefore, is consubstantial with, and equal to, the Father and the Son.

The *Filioque*

The term *filioque* means "and the Son" in Latin. The Cappadocian or Eastern Orthodox trinitarian theology maintains that the Holy Spirit proceeds from the Father alone. The Western Latin theology teaches that the Spirit proceeds from the Father "and the Son." This discord in trinitarian theology has been a source of great division between the Orthodox and Catholic Churches, not so much based on theological disagreement, but based on the fact that the Catholic Church unilaterally and illegitimately inserted the *filioque* into the Creed. The *filioque* is, in the strongest terms, an interpolation of the Creed formulated at the Ecumenical Councils of Nicaea (325 A.D.) and of Constantinople (381 A.D.). Because the Creed is by definition the universal expression of the faith and the recognizable symbol of unity, it may be altered or amended licitly only by another Ecumenical Council. Therefore, the unilateral interpolation of the Creed by the Western Church before the Great Schism (progressively from 1054-1204) was unjustifiable.⁹⁹ In 810 Pope Leo III emphatically rejected the corruption of the Creed (even though

---

⁹⁷ Hayes, *Mystery of the Trinity*, 55.
⁹⁸ *Breviloquium*, I.3:9.
⁹⁹ For a brief history of the *filioque*, see Timothy (Callistos) Ware, *The Orthodox Church* (New York: Penguin Books, 1963); John Meyendorff, *Byzantine Theology: Historical Trends and Doctrinal Themes* (New York: Fordham University Press, 1979); Corinne Winter, "Filioque" in *The HarperCollins Encyclopedia of Catholicism*, First Edition (San Francisco: Harper Collins, 1995).

he thought the *filioque* to be sound theology). The interpolation began in Spain (at the Council of Toledo in 589) and spread to France and Germany. By 1014 Rome succumbed when Pope Benedict VIII approved the interpolated Creed.

Apart from the fact that the *filioque* is an interpolation to the Creed, it is nevertheless good and sound trinitarian theology because it is faithful to what we know about the Trinity as it is revealed in the history of salvation. Because Bonaventure's trinitarian theology is Cappadocian, it could provide the Catholic Church with an excellent resource from which to dialogue with our Orthodox brothers and sisters on the matter of the *filioque*.

However, Bonaventure is not Cappadocian with regard to the *filioque*; he follows Augustine who holds that the Spirit proceeds from the Father and the Son. In order to distinguish the persons, Augustine needs to designate each one's personal property. The persons are distinguished by the processions which, for Augustine, are the opposite relations (within the divine substance): the Father is the one who generates the Son. The Son is the one generated by the Father. What is the opposing relation for the Spirit? What is the relation of the Spirit to the Son? Thus, Augustine calls the Spirit "Gift," so that Gift is opposed to Giver (Father and Son together).[100] Augustine explains that the Spirit proceeds from the Father (John 15:26), but is also called "the Spirit of Christ" (Rom 8:9). Therefore, it is clear that the Spirit is the Spirit of both the Father and of the Son. This denotes to whom the Spirit belongs, and is, therefore, a relation.

Since the relationship is not apparent in the name "Spirit," it is revealed when the Spirit is called Gift of God (Cf. Acts 8:20), being the Gift of the Father and the Son. We may, therefore, speak of "the gift of the giver and the giver of the gift," whereby we express a mutual and opposite relationship.[101] Augustine is the first to call the Spirit Love (insofar as "God is love," 1 John 4:8), because it is Love who joins the Father and the Son, and who joins us to them.[102] Bonaventure also calls the Spirit

---

[100] LaCugna, *God For Us*, 90.

[101] Augustine, *The Trinity*, V:11-12, *Fathers of the Church* 45, 189-91. Cf. Yves Congar, *I Believe in the Holy Spirit* I (New York: Seabury Press, 1983), 79-80.

[102] Augustine, *The Trinity*, VII: 3-6. *Fathers of the Church* 45, 225-41.

"Gift" and "Love," and while he received this tradition from Augustine, these designations function differently in his trinitarian framework. He has no need of finding an opposing set of relations within the divine substance in order to distinguish the person of the Spirit. His emphasis is on the person of the Father (not on the substance) as the Unbegotten Source from whom the persons proceed, and from whom the relations are derived, as in Cappadocian theology, i.e., from origin (not "oppositions"). Because of Bonaventure's unique trinitarian framework which is Cappadocian, with the *filioque*, "Gift" and "Bond" indicate much more of a unifying principle (whereas in Augustine, the term Gift designates an opposite relation).

The *filioque* is essential to Bonaventure's trinitarian theology as a whole. The belief that the Spirit proceeds from the Father and the Son functions in four ways in his theology:

1. The *filioque* means that there is in the Trinity the highest communication or sharing of being possible; the Father withholds nothing from the Son and communicates even the property of producing the Spirit.
2. The *filioque* is a formulation of a theology based on what God reveals about Godself in history; it strengthens the tie between what is said about the inner life of the Trinity and the Trinity revealed in history.
3. The *filioque* is necessary for the Word to be comprehensively the *Persona Media*.
4. The *filioque* distinguishes the Persons of the Son and the Spirit further than simply to label their processions "generation" and "spiration."

THE HIGHEST SELF-COMMUNICATION

The generation of the Son is the Father's perfect, absolute, infinite, and eternal *Self*-giving, and so nothing is withheld that can logically be shared, not even the property of production. When we say that the Father begets or produces or generates the Son, we are referring to a complete *self*-communication of Being, divine life, Goodness, in short, *ALL* that God is. Utterly unlike human generation, the generation of the Son does not result in a new being, but eternally produces "one in [the same] Being with the Father," (*homoousios* in original Greek language of the Creed). The Son, therefore, is perfectly equal to the Father; there could be no hint of subordination.[103] This generous self-emptying of the Father is the fullest realization of divine self-diffusive goodness. If the property of production were not eternally shared in the diffusion of the Son, then a greater self-diffusion could be imagined, and therefore, this would not be the highest good.

The argument against the *filioque* has been that it weakens the *monarchia* of the Father, the belief that the Father is the single Source of divinity. If Bonaventure's trinitarian theology is Greek, how can the *filioque* not undermine the whole trinitarian model? Cappadocian trinitarian theology predicated the *monarchia* of the Father. "Monarchy" has negative connotations today; the shades of meaning for words change over long periods of time and across cultures. The Greek word *arche* (from *mone arche*) should be understood in its meaning of "principle," rather than its meaning of "rule." There has never been any trinitarian exposition about the "rule" of the Father in the Trinity, but only about the Father as eternal Principle, Source, or Origin. Even if the word "principle" implies that it is greater than its issue, this cannot be the case in the Trinity, as the full equality of the Son and Spirit have been repeatedly defended. After all, there is no *real* priority in eternity.

THE *FILIOQUE* AND THE HISTORY OF SALVATION

Almost all the arguments in favor of the *filioque* which Bonaventure offers in the *Sentences*[104] are drawn from salvation

---

[103] The original intent of the *filioque* was to overcome Arianism, a form of subordinationism that held that Jesus was divine but not equal in attributes with the Father.

[104] I Sent., d.11, a.u., q.1.

history. According to the Gospel of John (John 15:26; John 16:7; John 16:12-15), the Spirit is called the Spirit of both the Father and the Son; and, arguably, is sent by both the Father and the Son. In Galatians, Paul says that "God has sent the Spirit of his Son into our hearts, crying, 'Abba! Father!'"(Gal 4:6). If it is God*self* (and not something other than God) that is revealed in the story of salvation, then the historical missions are manifestations of the eternal emanations. The *filioque* could not be more in accord with Bonaventure's whole theological system in which the Trinity is utterly inseparable from salvation history.

It must be granted that he devotes an extraordinary amount of philosophical speculation to the immanent Trinity's personal life, i.e. processional origins, personal relations, who means what to whom (Word, Image, Gift, Love), the reasons for plurality in God, and the reasons there must be three, and only three, persons, etc. Nevertheless, it must also be admitted that Bonaventure's doctrine of exemplarity understood in its full and cosmic scope, as well as the role the Word plays in this doctrine as *persona media*, serve to bind his trinitarian speculations tightly to *God*'s activity in the history of salvation. All creation for Bonaventure bears an imprint (vestige) of the Trinity, reflecting and proclaiming God's power, wisdom, and goodness, as appropriated to the Father, Son, and Spirit, respectively. If the whole universe is an entirely free expression of God's *inner* fecundity, goodness, and love, then it is logical to understand that the divine missions in the world are the historical manifestations of the emanations within Godself.[105] "Mission" does not imply any form of subordination; it is meant to connote origin and relation. The one who sends is not greater than those sent. The will and the work of the Trinity is one. "To say that the 'Father sends the Son' is equivalent to saying that he manifests the emanation of the Son; to say that 'the Son is sent' is equivalent to saying that in an historical effect it is made known that the Son emanates from another."[106]

---

[105] I Sent., d.15, p.1, a.u., q.3, 262-63.
[106] *Mystery of the Trinity*, 64 n146.

The *Filioque* and the *Persona Media*

If the Spirit does not proceed from the Father and the Son, then the Son cannot be understood comprehensively as the *Persona Media*. The Second Person of the Trinity would not be known as the one who both is produced and produces, who both receives and gives divine life, who is both active and passive, who both processes forth and is the origin of another. All the logical possibilities of production would not be exhausted, and the "necessary reasons" for three persons, no more and no less, would be entirely undermined. Christ the *Center* of history, creation, the Christian life, and the means by which we return to God, would not have his preexistent and eternal foundation in the Word who is the *Center* of the Trinity. If the Spirit does not proceed from the Father and the Son, then there would be no correspondence between the Word's central role in intra-divine life and the Word's historical incarnate mission.

The love with which the Father loves the Son, and the Son, in turn, loves the Father, would not be the person of the Holy Spirit—if the Spirit could not proceed from the Son, for the Spirit could not be called the love of the Son, nor the bond of love between the Father and the Son, nor their mutual gift. Divine life could not be metaphorically described as a divine circular "dance," for the Spirit could not "close the circle" of self-transcending love from the Son back to the Father. Instead of an eternal circle of divine life-giving love, the imaginative configuration of the processions would look more like (geometrical) rays diverging from a single vertex, the Father.

The Distinction Between the Son and Spirit

If the Spirit does not proceed from the Father and the Son as one principle, then what distinguishes the Son from the Spirit? If both proceed from the Father alone, what is the difference in their manner of procession? Of course, one could respond by saying that one is generated, and is therefore the Son; and the other is spirated, and is therefore the Spirit. If generation and procession both mean they "come forth from another," what distinguishes the two manners of being produced? The *filioque* distinguishes the spiration of the Spirit as the mode of procession from the Father and the Son as one origin, rather than the procession from the Father alone. The *filioque*, however, should not be labeled the "double procession," as Orthodox Christians do. The Holy Spirit does not proceed twice, nor even once, but eternally. There are *not* two principles in the Trinity, but one, the Father, the fontal-overflowing Source from whom all divine life proceeds eternally. The Son and the Father breathe forth the Spirit as one principle. Certainly, if we profess one God, that is, one "center of consciousness," and say that there is one will, one intellect, one energy or operation in God when we are referring to the three divine Persons, then surely the Father and the Son, as two Persons, can be understood as the one principle of the Holy Spirit. If we can say, "the Three are One," we can surely say, "the Two are One."

THE UNITY OF THE TRINITY: THE SINGLE DIVINE NATURE

Bonaventure shows concern for securing the divine unity of the Trinity throughout his works. It is a coextensive concern with that of divine plurality in the *Disputed Questions on the Mystery of the Trinity*. In *The Soul's Journey into God* the chapter on God's unity precedes his inimitable chapter on the divine Persons. Bonaventure's work is quite balanced with regard to unity of being and plurality of persons.

In both the *Mystery of the Trinity* and the *Soul's Journey*, Bonaventure grounds his arguments in Scripture,[107] which, he says, is all that is needed regarding this question, but he wishes to demonstrate it by the use of reason.[108] Throughout the entire

---

[107] For the *Mystery of the Trinity*: Ex 20:2: "God, your God is one"; Deut 6:4 and 32:39: "I alone am God, and there is no other God beside me"; Ps 80:10 "You shall not worship any foreign God." For the *Soul's Journey*: Ex 3:14: "I am who am."

[108] *Mystery of the Trinity*, II:1.

Mystery of the Trinity he explicitly relies on Anselm's[109] insight that God is "the highest Being than which no greater can be conceived."[110] Thus, the divine Being is one, and a plurality of persons does not multiply the divine nature. Production does not multiply the divine nature. A plurality of three persons does not mean there are three "centers of consciousness" in the Trinity; no one holds this tri-theistic position. There is one divine nature, one intellect, one will, one activity or operation, and so there is one God.

Each Person Unifies the Trinity

Bonaventure maintains the traditional position that the single divine substance (or being) unifies the divine Persons, but Bonaventure's trinitarian theology is unique in that divine unity is grounded *not only* in the divine substance, but also, in a distinct way, in *each* of the Persons. Any way one looks at his model of the Trinity, one finds a unifying principle.

The Father is the unifying principle in the Cappadocian Trinity. As the **Un**originate Origin of all being, both divine and non-divine, the Father is the unifying Source of the Trinity. Of course, the Greeks confess the trinitarian formula "one Being in three Persons" (*mia ousia, treis hypostaseis*), but the "divine Being" is utterly unthinkable *apart* from the Persons. The three persons do not *have* a common Being, they *are* the divine Being.[111] This distinction may seem minor, but in reality, it is an entirely different mentality. The Greek proposition takes seriously that God's being is incomprehensible, altogether unapproachable.

Bonaventure *does* have an understanding of the divine substance as held by the Augustinian tradition. Although he demonstrates a familiarity with it, it does not dominate his trinitarian approach in the least. He is conversant with both trinitarian

---

[109] Anselm, *Proslogion*, 3:4 and 15 in *St. Anselm: Basic Writings* (LaSalle, IL: Open Court Publishing, 1962).

[110] *Mystery of the Trinity*, I.1:22-26.

[111] LaCugna, *God For Us*, 192. Emphasis in original.

approaches. The point here is that the Cappadocian position on the Father as the Source of unity in the Trinity is inherited along with the Greek trinitarian model and is evident in Bonaventure's theology, although clearly not in its full strength, the *filioque* notwithstanding. As we recall, the position of the Father as the unoriginate fontal-overflowing fecund Source of divinity has been well emphasized by Bonaventure and is pivotal to his understanding of the Trinity.

The Son's position as the *persona media* also unites the trinitarian Persons. As Ewert Cousins phrases it, "... the Father is the generating source, the *fontalis plenitudo*. At the opposite pole, the Holy Spirit is the person who is produced and does not produce, and hence can be called *spiratio passiva*. As Bonaventure observes, between these poles, there must be a *persona media*, *who contains the opposites within himself and thus holds the poles in union.*"[112] As we recall, the Son is *persona media* "in whom all things hold together" (Col 1:17) and, therefore, is a source of unity within the inner life of the Trinity.

The Spirit is called the Bond of Love between the Father and the Son. Within the Trinity this mutual love is a person, and this person unites the persons of the Trinity, not necessarily in a "logical" or "reasonable" way, but in the way that love unites. The Spirit needs very little explanation, as we all know something about the unitive nature of love. The Spirit as the Love which unites Father and Son can only be claimed if the Spirit proceeds from the Son and returns to the Father as their mutual Gift and Bond.

Circumincession

Circumincession corresponds to the Greek word *perichoresis* which originated with John of Damascus.[113] *Perichoresis* refers to the mutual indwelling of the trinitarian Persons, as revealed

---

[112] Cousins, *Bonaventure and the Coincidence of Opposites,* 138. Emphasis added.

[113] John of Damascus, *Exposition of the Orthodox Faith* (*De fide orthodoxa*) I.8 in Vol. IX of *Nicene and Post-Nicene Fathers* (Grand Rapids: Eerdmans, 1983).

by Christ's words, "I am in the Father and the Father is in me" (John 14:11). The Persons of the Trinity abide in each other eternally.

The concept of circumincession or mutual indwelling may be better understood through a simple exercise based on Augustine's "psychological trinity."[114] Augustine teaches that human beings are trinitarian images of the trinitarian God. We reflect God in our memory, intellect, and will. These triadic faculties are precisely what make us "human." Augustine correlates the human faculties to the Father, Son, and Holy Spirit, respectively. Each faculty is distinguishable from the others—remembering, thinking/knowing, and willing/choosing. I may ask questions regarding each faculty, e.g., Do you have a reliable memory? Do you have a strong intellect? Are you decisive in your choices when you exercise your will? In order to answer each question, you are required to think of each faculty distinctly. Yet the faculties are usually indivisible: You know what you will, and you will to know. And neither knowing nor willing is possible without a memory. (You exercise your will to remember something, and you remember what you will. You know what you remember, and you remember what you know.) The human faculties interpenetrate and mutually inhere to various degrees. I may ask you to recall a specific event: Do you remember your first day of school? If you wish to comply, your will moves your memory to call up the specific event, and you know the event you are remembering. The faculties are distinct (I can make you think about each one of them), but indivisible (you rarely use one without all three). They are united but unconfused.[115] The mutual indwelling of the human faculties is a limited and imperfect analogy for the mutual indwelling (circumincession) of the divine Persons. Yet, you have a direct experience of how

---

[114] Augustine, *On the Trinity*, Bk. X, The Fathers of the Church Series 45, 291-313. Bonaventure presents a more refined understanding of the soul as the trinitarian image of God, but according to the Cappadocian model, not Augustine's model, in *The Soul's Journey*, ch. 3.

[115] John of Damascus used the formula "united, yet unconfused; distinct, yet undivided" to describe the trinitarian Persons, *Exposition of the Orthodox Faith*, I:8. I use it to describe our triadic faculties.

three faculties are one soul. This experience may give you some limited insight of how three Persons are one God.

Bonaventure's understanding of divine circumincession is dynamic, consonant with eternal self-giving, self-emptying, self-transcending divine love. Unlike the Greek conception of the *perichoretic* activity, the intra-trinitarian movement is circular in that there is an eternal reciprocation of the Son's love to the Father. This love between them is the Spirit. It is the circular dance of divine love.

In the Augustinian/Thomistic model of the Trinity the doctrine of circumincession is superfluous because the Trinity is already understood as one single divine substance in which the three Persons subsist. Because Bonaventure's trinitarian theology is Cappadocian, he is the only one in the Latin West who would have any real use for the doctrine of circumincession. It is not found even in the writings of his teacher, Alexander of Hales.[116] Bonaventure's understanding of intra-divine life is such that it is the Person of the Father (not the substance) who communicates Himself perfectly. In the *Commentary on the Sentences* he states:

> There is in the divine Persons supreme and perfect circumincession by reason of the unity of essence with the distinction of Persons ... it is called circumincession because each Person is in the others; and this is properly and perfectly only in God, because circumincession in being gives distinction and unity at the same time. And because there is the highest unity with distinction only in God, for this reason, the distinction is unconfused and unity is inseparable: hence for this reason, perfect circumincession exists in God alone. And the reason for this is clear, it is because circumincession is the perfect unity of essence with the distinction of Persons.[117]

---

[116] Jacques-Guy Bougerol, *Lexique Saint Bonaventure* (Paris: Editions Franciscaines, 1969), 34.

[117] I Sent., d.19, p.1, a.u., q.4, conclu., 349. Cf. also *The Collations*, 21:19.

In Bonaventure's trinitarian discussions there is a balanced emphasis on substance/essence and person; the balance is achieved without losing the understanding of the Persons' integral distinction in the sharing of the divine Being.

The various aspects of Bonaventure's model of the Trinity are very well integrated into a unique understanding, even though they come from different sources; for example, the Damascene's doctrine of *perichoresis* seems well suited to the Pseudo-Dionysian principle of self-diffusive goodness, as the quotation above demonstrates. These strands of doctrine are united with the Victorine principle of interpersonal love as the highest good, in order to produce Bonaventure's "well-rounded" and cogent trinitarian model.

BONAVENTURE: THE FRANCISCAN RESOURCE FOR THEOLOGICAL QUESTIONS TODAY

In Bonaventure's work the Franciscan tradition offers the entire Christian Church a comprehensive and highly developed trinitarian theology that is faithful to divine revelation because it makes assertions about the triune nature of God on the basis of salvation history, drawn from God's self-revelation through Christ and in the Spirit. The distinctively Franciscan insight in Bonaventure's theology is his central emphasis that God is fecund, fontal-overflowing Goodness and Love, and therefore God is a communion of three equal Persons who dwell in eternal, ecstatic, kenotic, self-transcending, interdependent, and mutual love. In conclusion, it is important to name some specific areas where this theology of the Trinity is a resource for our understanding of human life, the mission of the Christian, the nature of the Church, the use of language, and our understanding of creation.

(1) Human beings are created in the image and likeness of God (Gen 1:27). This is not some quaint, biblical cliché; this is at the heart of our theological anthropology. We image God in our capacity to know and to love. We reflect the tri-Personal God most clearly in generous and self-transcending relationships.

The Bonaventurian understanding of the Trinity is of incalculable worth as a model for human interpersonal relations, because it offers us values that are indispensable to authentic human community: equality and non-subordination, reciprocity, interdependence, inclusivity, generosity, mutual self-donation, and dynamic productivity. Such a view of human community has implications for how our institutions and sharing of goods reflect our core belief in the Trinity.

(2) Along this vein of thought, Bonaventure's Trinity is a tremendous resource for feminist trinitarian theology that raises the question of whether referring to God exclusively as Father, Son, and Spirit is too patriarchal and oppressive to women. God is not literally a "father." Fathers are male; they normally require mothers to be fathers; and they are links in a generational chain, i.e., every father is also a son. God the Father is not male and is beyond gender, does not have a mate, and does not originate from another (as Bonaventure argues, God the Father's distinguishing property is Unbegottenness or *Innascibilitas* and being the Unoriginate Origin). Jesus called God Father because the appellation approximates most closely their ineffably intimate and trusting relationship based on eternal *origin*, which distinguishes the First and Second Person, i.e. one comes from the other eternally. We can employ gender-neutral, though completely accurate, terms for the Trinity by saying that God is the Parental Person who produces the Filial Person, and together they breathe forth the Pneumatic Person. However, for all its use of the word "Person," this trinitarian formulation seems impersonal, loveless, clinical, and unrelated to us. Because the Father-Son-Spirit metaphor is the one Jesus used to disclose his relationships within the Godhead, it is preeminent and formulaic in our referring to God.

God's fatherhood must always be understood in non-literal, non-patriarchal, and non-idolatrous ways.[118] Bonaventure's theology authentically interprets the term "Father" as an indication of intimacy, mutuality, and relationality based on eternal

---

[118] See Maria Calisi, "Bonaventure's Trinitarian Theology as a Feminist Resource," *Spirit and Life* 8 (1999), 117-32.

origin, and authentically understands the Father's "primacy" as fecundity.

Bonaventure never hesitates to use many and original names for the trinitarian Persons, e.g. *Fontalis Plentitudo*, Unbegotten Source, Unoriginate Origin, and Creator for the Parental Person; Word, Image, Likeness, Exemplar, and *Persona Media* for the Filial Person; and Love, Gift, Bond of Love for the Pneumatic Person. A theology such as this serves as an example of a theology deeply rooted in the Christian Tradition, yet open to the feminist Christian question of the exclusive use of male metaphors for God.

(3) Furthermore, because of Bonaventure's doctrine of exemplarity, the Franciscan understanding of the Trinity is never separate nor *separable* from other Christian teachings on creation, the Incarnation, redemption, Christian anthropology, and spirituality.[119] Bonaventure's understanding of the Trinity makes it the central Christian doctrine.

(4) Bonaventure's trinitarian theology may be a solid starting point for dialogue between the Catholic and Orthodox Churches on the question of the *filioque* (that the Spirit proceeds from the Father *"and the Son"*). The *filioque* may be a somewhat theologically technical and obscure point to most Christians of all denominations, but it is not trivial. The Creed is our Symbol of Christian unity and our confession of Christian faith. An understanding of the divine inter-Personal relations is at the heart of understanding who God is and how God comes to us as Son and Spirit. The Orthodox Church's major problem with the *filioque* is that it presents a "double procession," as they call it. For Orthodox Christians the *filioque* seems to posit two Sources from which the Spirit proceeds. It destroys the "monarchy of

---

[119] The first four volumes of The Franciscan Heritage Series, of which *Trinitarian Perspectives* is a part, deal with Christian doctrines that are related to the Trinity. See volumes One through Four: *The Franciscan Intellectual Tradition: Tracing Its Origins and Identifying Its Central Components* by Kenan Osborne (2003); *The Franciscan View of Creation: Learning to Live in a Sacramental World* by Ilia Delio (2003); *The Franciscan View of the Human Person: Some Central Elements* by Dawn M. Nothwehr (2005); and *The Franciscan Vision and the Gospel of John: The San Damiano Cross* by Michael D. Guinan (2006) published by Franciscan Institute Publications.

the Father," or the Father's unique, distinguishing property of being the sole eternal Source of divinity. The Father is the unifying principle in the Orthodox model of the Trinity. There is one God because there is one Father. For Bonaventure the Father is uniquely the Unbegotten One. Unbegottenness (not coming from another) remains the fecund, uncommunicable, and distinguishing property that establishes the Father as the *Fontalis Plenitudo* and sole eternal Source of divinity. In Bonaventure's model of Trinity there is no question of a "double procession," because his model upholds the "monarchy of the Father," in the only authentic understanding of the word "monarchy," namely, "single source" (and not "single rule").

(5) Lastly, Bonaventure's interpretation of primacy and monarchy emphasizes not rule but relationality and fecundity. This may provide a theological vision capable of fostering another mode of leadership in the Church, one which establishes its credibility through its encouragement of participation, mutual exchange, the promotion of the "other" and the witness to communion.

Part II: Bonaventure, Francis, and the Experience of the Tri-Personal God

Introduction

In contrast to Bonaventure and all trinitarian theological discourse, Francis did not understand the Trinity in philosophical categories. He was not trained as a scholastic or "schoolman." Francis had a deep and abiding consciousness of God in his life, and this experience of God was tri-Personal. He prayed to God the Father, through the Son whom he emulated with every breath, in the power of Holy Spirit who inspired and led him.

The idea of contemplating the Trinity as "God in Godself" would have seemed alien to Francis. What would be the point? Why would one want to know *about* God, when one had been called to *know* God? Above all else, Francis knew God's love. He experienced God's love intimately in the overflowing divine generosity he found in creation, in the Incarnation, in the Passion, and in the enduring joy that comes with imitating Christ.

As we have seen, the most important insight of Bonaventure's Franciscan trinitarian theology is the emphasis on the infinite love and goodness of God. He integrates this essential Franciscan emphasis into his theological system by using the Dionysian principle of the self-diffusive nature of the good. God's love is experienced as overwhelming generosity in the diversity and majesty of creation and in the stunning divine humility of the Incarnation and Passion. Bonaventure articulates this divine generosity in his metaphor of *fontalis plenitudo* (fountain-fullness) and the absolute fecundity as Unbegotten Source. Generosity may be defined as the desire to share what one has, and what God shares is being and life. No higher state of being can be conceived than a life of shared love, and personhood (or relationality) is necessary for the perfection of love.

In order to articulate Francis's experience of a God who is so lovingly and intensely personal that he deigned to become human, Bonaventure turned to the work of Richard of St. Victor for a theology of interpersonal relationships, rather than to Augustine's theology of opposite and mutual relations *within* the divine substance. The Christocentric life that Francis lived daily was translated into the *persona media* within the Trinity, between the Trinity and creation, and in the history of salvation. Francis's mystical experience of God in and through all creation found an expressive outlet in Bonaventure's doctrine of exemplarity wherein God is reflected as triune. This doctrine of exemplarity reinforces the intense relationality of God to the world and to us. In Bonaventure's trinitarian theology, as well as in his whole theological system, God can never be viewed as unrelated to the world, but rather as freely and deeply involved in human life and in all of creation. These distinctive theological formulations of Franciscan trinitarian theology are based on the original personal insights of Francis himself who experienced God in a unique and privileged way, and who, in turn, witnessed to this experience of God in everyday life.

Seeing this connection between Bonaventure's scholastic theology and Francis's spiritual experience is important. It establishes a continuity of vision, practice, and mission at the heart of the Franciscan intellectual tradition. In the second part of this reflection, I would like to elaborate on these fundamental connections in two ways: first, by showing how Bonaventure tried to communicate a practical spirituality of the Trinity, especially the experience of the Holy Spirit, by presenting a model of participation in trinitarian life in his *Legend of St. Francis*; and second, by examining the Trinitarian vision which Francis reflected in his own writings. Perhaps Bonaventure and Francis in this way might jointly mirror for us a way to appropriate our Trinitarian belief at the center of our life and mission.

Bonaventure's *Major Legend of Saint Francis* (*The Life of Blessed Francis*)

God comes to us in history through Christ and in the Spirit, and we respond and return to God whom we now call Father in the same way, through Christ and in the Spirit. Bonaventure's *Major Legend of Saint Francis*,[120] his biography of Francis, demonstrates that this structure for salvation in history is paradigmatic in Francis's individual life. In turning to the *Major Legend* in our search for Franciscan insights on the Trinity, we must approach the work carefully, and with a full consciousness that it is *Bonaventure's* hagiographical *interpretation* of Francis's life.[121] It cannot be read as a literal, historical account of events, including the accounts of the Spirit's movements in Francis's life. However, when we study Francis's own writings, we find that Bonaventure may not have been far from the mark in articulating Francis's experience of the tri-Personal God and of the Spirit's role in particular.

In the biographies of Francis the central role of Christ in his life cannot be overstated. Francis imitated Christ to the extreme, especially in his espousal of poverty, his practice of humility and obedience, his preaching repentance and the Good News, his inexhaustible love for God and neighbor, and his acceptance of transformative suffering. It is through Christ the Son that Francis came to know the Father, but it is by the power of the Holy Spirit, as Bonaventure presents it, that Francis was inspired to follow Christ. The Holy Spirit has a similar but minimal role in Thomas of Celano's *Life of Saint Francis*.[122] Bonaventure explic-

---

[120] Bonaventure, *The Major Legend of Saint Francis* (*The Life of Blessed Francis*) in FAED 2.

[121] *The Major Legend*, Bonaventure's hagiographical interpretation of Francis, is based on two sources: the biographies by Thomas of Celano and by Julian of Speyer, as well as Bonaventure's own interviews with Francis's surviving companions. Cf. Ewert Cousins, *Bonaventure: The Life of St. Francis*, "Introduction," 38-39.

[122] See the role of the Holy Spirit in Thomas of Celano's *Life of Saint Francis*: I.4.8; I.11.26; I.12.31; I.15.36; I.18.47 and 48; I.29.80; II.2.92; in *Francis of Assisi: Early Documents*, Vol. I: *The Saint*, ed. Regis J. Armstrong, J.A. Wayne Hellmann, and William J. Short (Hyde Park, NY: New City Press, 1999) and will be referred to as FAED 1 followed by the page number.

itly mentions or indirectly alludes to the activity of the Holy Spirit no less than forty-three times in the *Major Legend*. He depicts the Spirit's activity explicitly in Francis's life twenty-seven times and uses the word "inspiration" (alone) four times; he alludes indirectly to the Spirit's activity another seven times and even portrays the Holy Spirit overflowing beyond Francis to work upon his contemporaries six times.

In salvation history, God the Father never "descends," so to speak, but sends the Son and Spirit whom Irenaeus called God's right and left hands that do God's work in creation.[123] Jesus sent his Spirit, or asked the Father to send the Spirit, after his Resurrection at Pentecost, but in many ways the Spirit preceded the coming of Christ: The life-giving Spirit of God was active in creating the universe, spoke through the prophets, and conceived Jesus in Mary's womb. The Holy Spirit is God ever-present, vivifying, animating, and dynamically renewing creation and human hearts. The Holy Spirit descended upon Jesus at his baptism (Matt 3:13-17; Mark 1:10-11; Luke 3:21-22; John 1:29-34), "led" or "drove" him into the wilderness to fast and pray (Luke 4:1 and Mark 1:12, respectively), empowered him to start his public ministry (Luke 4:14), anointed him as Messiah to proclaim the Good News (Luke 4:18; Cf. Is 61:1- 2; 58:6), and caused him to rejoice (Luke 10:21). Jesus encouraged his hearers to ask the Father to give the Spirit (Luke 11:13), and assured them that the Spirit would teach them what to say to their adversaries (Luke 12:12).

In ways similar to the activity of the Spirit in relation to Christ in the Gospels, Bonaventure's depiction of the Spirit's activity upon Francis, who had genuinely opened himself to it, is reminiscent of the "Spirit Christology." The Holy Spirit both prepared Francis for anointing and anointed him,[124] "led" him

---

[123] Irenaeus, *Against the Heresies*, IV, pref., 4; also V, 6.1 in *The Ante-Nicene Fathers*, vol. I, trans. Alexander Roberts and James Donaldson (Grand Rapids: Eerdmans, 1985).

[124] *Major Legend*, 1:2; 4:4; 11:2; 12:7 in FAED 2, 531-32; 551-52; 613-14; 625-26.

to go away to fast and pray,[125] empowered him to preach the Gospel,[126] taught him,[127] caused him consolation[128] and joy.[129] It is the inspiration and power of the Holy Spirit that allowed Francis to imitate Christ so perfectly and to make Christ the center of his life, as all the biographies portray.

The Holy Spirit was also poured out and "filled" those who sought God's will in the early chapters of Luke: besides Mary, of course, there were Elizabeth, John in her womb, Zechariah, and Simeon (Luke 1:35; 1:41; 1:67; and 2:25, respectively). Similarly, the Spirit overflowed upon Francis's contemporaries; these include the five men who were called by the Spirit to be among the early friars; John of St. Paul, Bishop of Sabina, who was inspired to argue Francis's case for the Order's Rule to Pope Innocent III; Pope Innocent himself in confirming the Rule; the friars at the provincial chapter; the friar who was especially devoted to Francis; Brother Silvester, and Clare.[130]

A biographer may or may not explicitly present the Spirit's activity, as Bonaventure does, but this *is* the (often unnoted) paradigm of the Christian life: the Spirit inspires and empowers us to follow Christ to the Father.

---

[125] *Major Legend*, 2:1; 4.11; 10:2; 10:3 in FAED 2, 536-37; 557-59; 606; 625-26. The Spirit inspired Francis to go into San Damiano to pray where he heard Christ's command to repair his house. (*Major Legend*, 2:1 in FAED 2, 536-37).

[126] *Major Legend*, 3:2; 4:5; 12:7 in FAED 2, 543; 553; 625-26. Cf. Matt 9:35; Luke 9:60; 1 Cor 2:4, 13.

[127] *Major Legend*, 2:1; 11:2; 11:14; 12:12 in FAED 2, 536-37; 613-14; 620-21; 628-29. In *The Major Legend*, 4:11 the Spirit inspired the Rule. Francis was given divine utterance to speak to the Saracen commander, the Soldan of Babylon (*Major Legend* 9:7-8 in FAED 2, 601-03) and to preach to Pope Honorius III and cardinals when he invoked the Holy Spirit (*Major Legend* 12.7 in FAED 2, 625-26). Cf. Luke 12:12 and 21:15.

[128] *Major Legend*, 3:3 in FAED 2, 543-44.

[129] *Major Legend*, 3:6 in FAED 2, 545.

[130] *Major Legend*, 3:4; 3:9; 3:10; 4:10; 11:9; 12:2, in FAED 2, 544; 547-48; 548-49; 557; 617-18; 623-24, respectively.

Francis's Own Writings[131]

Based on his writings, it may be said that Francis has a trinitarian consciousness or "mindfulness" of God, for he speaks of the Father, Son, and Spirit most often, and rarely speaks of God as simply "God." Francis was not trained in theology, nor conversant with the philosophical categories that professional theologians used to discuss the Trinity. The Holy Trinity for Francis is not an abstract formulation of faith, but a dynamic, life-giving, and intensely personal reality at work in his life. His articulation of his experience of God may be described as a trinitarian theology "from below." Rather than speaking about the Trinity by beginning with the eternal inner life of God apart from us, i.e., trinitarian theology "from above," Francis speaks about the Trinity "from below," based on experiential and intimate knowledge which he expresses in the language of Scripture.

Francis's writings are drenched with Gospel quotations and allusions. Faithful to both the Gospel message and to his own personal experience, the salient feature in his articulation of the Trinity's presence is that God is love and goodness (the two are interchangeable or convertible). Just as the most unique and distinctive principle of Bonaventure's trinitarian theology is the self-diffusiveness of the good, the most striking element of Francis's trinitarian references (as well as most of his writings) is the love and goodness of God. Even if the Franciscan tradition did not have all the other distinctive features—the primacy/fecundity of the Father, God's relatedness to the world through exemplarity, the centrality of Christ as the *Persona Media*, and the emphasis on self-transcending, interpersonal relationships within the Trinity—even without all of these, the resounding message that God is overflowing love and goodness would be

---

[131] There is debate about whether or not Francis actually composed the documents attributed to him. Here I am using Francis's writings in an integral way and not addressing the question of composition or authorship. For critical reflections, see Francesco d'Assisi, *Scritti, Testo latino e traduzione italiana* (Milano: Editrici Francescane, 2002); Giovanni Miccoli, "The Writings of Francis," *Greyfriars Review* 15 (2001): 135-70; Carlo Paolazzi, "Francis and His Use of Scribes: A Puzzle to Scholars," *Greyfriars Review* 18 (2004): 323-41.

the most indispensable and worthwhile contribution that any theological tradition could make to trinitarian theology.

Francis directs his prayers to God the Father through Christ the Son in the power of the Holy Spirit. He calls the Father "good:" "You are the most high, ... You are the good, all good, the highest good, ... You are love, charity."[132] In another prayer, he addresses God as "... most high and supreme God: all good, supreme good, totally good, You Who *alone are good*."[133] Yet again in a *Prayer Inspired by the Our Father*, Francis prays "You, Lord, are Love, ... You, Lord, are the Supreme Good, the Eternal Good, from Whom all good comes, without Whom there is no good."[134] The tone of prayerful exuberance and ecstatic praise is unmistakable. There is a build up of emotion in addressing God who is so overwhelmingly good. It is this boundless goodness of God that attracted Francis to seek God always and everywhere. God is lavishly, unreservedly, and indiscriminately good to have created the universe, become flesh, suffered, died, and rose from the dead to save abject sinners, all through the Son and by the power of the Spirit. God's goodness permeates all reality, for Francis, and it starts with the Father.

God is also love,[135] and Francis repeatedly, and with heartfelt conviction, exhorts the friars and the faithful to love God above all else,[136] to love our neighbors,[137] and to love even our enemies[138] (quoting the relevant scriptural passages).

---

[132] Francis of Assisi, *The Praises of God and the Blessing* (*The Parchment Given to Brother Leo on La Verna*), 2, 3 and 4 in FAED 1, 109-12.

[133] *The Praises To Be Said at All the Hours*, 11 in FAED 1, 162.

[134] *Prayer Inspired by the Our Father*, 2 in FAED 1, 158. God is described in very similar words in *The Earlier Rule*, 17:17 and in 23:9 in FAED 1, 76, 85: "Who is the fullness of good, all good, every good, the true and supreme good. Who alone is good ..."

[135] *Earlier Exhortation to the Brothers and Sisters of Penance* (*The First Version of the Letter to the Faithful*), 2:19; *The Praises of God*, 4; *Our Father*, 2; *Earlier Rule*, 17:5 in FAED 1, 44; 109; 158; 75.

[136] *The Earlier Rule*, 11:5-6 and 23:8; *Admonition*, 20; *Earlier Exhortation*, 1:1; *Later Admonition and Exhortation to the Brothers and Sisters of Penance* (*Second Version of the Letter to the Faithful*), 1, 18, and 19 in FAED 1, 72; 84; 135; 41; 45-46.

[137] *Earlier Rule*, 11:5; *Earlier Exhortation*, 1:1; *Later Admonition*, 26-27, and 30 in FAED 1, 72; 41; 47.

[138] *Admonition* 9; *Later Admonition*, 38 in FAED 1, 132, 48.

Although Francis does not use these words, God is infinite and transcendent goodness; God's goodness is beyond anything we finite beings can conceive of goodness. There is, therefore, a sense that God is "distant" or transcendent. For Francis God is "Most High,"[139] a term he repeatedly uses. Yet God is "most high" *because* God is all-good; God is great *because* God is Goodness. Francis could attest to this by direct experience. He expresses his consciousness of God the Father in the first of his *Admonitions* by quoting Jesus' prayer to the Father in John's Gospel:

> The Lord Jesus says to his disciples: "I am the way, the truth and the life; no one comes to the Father except through me...." The Father dwells in inaccessible light (cf. 1Tim 6:16), and God is spirit (John 4:24), and no one has ever seen God (John 1:18). Therefore He cannot be seen except in the Spirit ... But because He is equal to the Father, the Son is not seen by anyone other than the Father or other than the Holy Spirit.[140]

There is a sense that God the Father is Holy Mystery—transcendent, unattainable, and inaccessible, except through the Son and Spirit. God is "made" accessible through Christ who is the way to God who "cannot be seen except in the Spirit."

God is exceedingly worthy of all praise, adoration, and glory. The Father is the high and almighty King,[141] the God of majesty, and the almighty Creator of the universe. God is beyond all things and we "are not worthy to pronounce [God's] name."[142] Nevertheless, much like Bonaventure, Francis does not hesitate simply to revel in naming the attributes of God. In a single prayer, Thaddée Matura has counted eighty-six divine qualities

---

[139] *Earlier Rule*, 17:17 and 23:11; *Admonition* 28; *Canticle of the Creatures* 1, 4 and 11; *A Letter to the Entire Order* 14, 52; *Office of the Passion*, Psalm 7.2; *Praises of God*, 2; *Prayer Before the Crucifix* in FAED 1, 76, 85-85; 137; 113-14; 117, 121; 147; 109; 40. Interestingly, Francis uses the term "Most High" to refer to Christ once in *Admonition* 1:10 in FAED 1, 128.

[140] *Admonition* 1:1-7 in FAED 1, 128.

[141] *Praises of God*, 2 in FAED 1, 109.

[142] *Earlier Rule*, 23:5; also *Canticle*, 2 in FAED 1, 82-83; 113.

that Francis used to praise God in direct address:[143] e.g., "You are three and one ... You are wisdom; You are humility; ... You are gladness and joy, You are our hope ... our sweetness ..."[144] Francis concludes his *Earlier Rule* with as many as fifty different descriptions of God: "... unchangeable, ... indescribable, ineffable, incomprehensible, unfathomable, blessed, ... glorious, ... most high, gentle, lovable ... delightful, and totally desirable above all else for ever."[145] Francis's expression of his consciousness of God travels from the most solemn reverential awe to outbursts of holy delight! God is the infinite, incomprehensible, all-powerful, almighty, Creator of the universe, *the Most High* whom Francis also calls "Father"[146] in direct address, and jubilantly exclaims "O how glorious and holy and great to have a Father in heaven!"[147]

PRIMACY OF THE FATHER

Just as the primacy of the Father is an important feature of Bonaventure's trinitarian theology, there is a certain primacy of the Father in Francis's writings as well. It is to God the Father that Francis usually addresses his prayers, just as the Son taught us to pray and indeed prayed himself.[148] The Father is the Source of all, of the Son and Spirit, of the universe, and of our salvation. This paternal primacy, or "monarchy" of the Fa-

---

[143] Matura's chapter on the Francis and the Trinity is comprehensive and excellent: Thaddée Matura, *Francis of Assisi: The Message in His Writings*, (St. Bonaventure, NY: Franciscan Institute Press, 1997; reprinted in 2004), 54. The prayer is *The Praises of God and the Blessing*. Among Francis's descriptions of God, Matura counts forty-one nouns and forty-five adjectives, "in an attempt to suggest something of God's ineffability."

[144] *Praises of God*, 3-5 in FAED 1, 109.

[145] *Earlier Rule*, 23:9-11 in FAED 1, 85-86; in Matura, *The Message in His Writings*, 54.

[146] *Earlier Exhortation*, 1:7; *Later Admonition* 21; *Our Father*, 1 in FAED 1, 41-42; 47; 158. Francis uses the terms "Holy Father" in *The Praises of God*, 2 and "holy and just Father" in *Earlier Rule*, 23:1 in FAED 1, 109; 81-82.

[147] *Later Admonition* 54 in FAED 1, 49.

[148] Two of Francis's fifteen prayers are addressed to Christ and two praise Mary his mother.

ther, is evident in chapter 23 of the *Earlier Rule* where Francis offers a prayer of praise and thanksgiving:

> All-powerful, most holy, almighty and supreme God, Holy and just Father, Lord King of heaven and earth, we thank You for Yourself for through Your holy will and through Your only Son with the Holy Spirit You have created everything spiritual and corporal and, after making us in Your own image and likeness, ... You brought about His birth as true God and true man ... and You willed to redeem us captives through His cross and blood and death.[149]

It is by the Father's will that the universe came to be, that we were created in the divine image, that the Son became human and that we are redeemed. In the same document Francis calls the Father our "Creator and Redeemer and Savior," which at first glance looks like a gender-neutral trinitarian formulation, but here the titles traditionally accorded to the Son, "Redeemer" and "Savior,"[150] are appropriated to the Father. He does something similar in the *Prayer Inspired by the Our Father*. Immediately after Francis addresses God as "our most holy Father," he augments it with "Our Creator, Redeemer, *Consoler*, and Savior."[151] Consoler is the name given to the Holy Spirit. This form of address for the Father is slightly unusual, but just as we say that the Father creates through the Son, so we may also say that the Father redeems and saves through the Son, and consoles through the Spirit. The Son and Spirit are "his hands" with whom he reaches out to us.

What is the proper response to such a benevolent God according to Francis?

---

[149] *Earlier Rule* 23:1 and 23:3 in FAED 1, 81-83.
[150] *Earlier Rule* 23:9 in FAED 1, 85. Francis calls the Son "Redeemer and Savior" directly in the *Earlier Rule*, 16:7 in FAED 1, 74, and he concludes *The Praises of God and The Blessing* by calling God the Father "Merciful Savior" which usually designates Christ in FAED 1, 109. In the Magnificat (Luke 1:47), Mary rejoices "in God my Savior."
[151] *Our Father* 1 in FAED 1, 158.

> With our whole heart, our whole soul, our whole mind, with our whole strength and fortitude, with our whole understanding, with all our powers, with every effort, every affection, every feeling, every desire and wish let us all love the Lord God ... Who has created, redeemed and will save us by His mercy alone, Who did and does everything good for us...[152]

Francis is unequivocal and unrestrained in augmenting the biblical description of how we should love God in return. Note that he repeats how he understands the activity of the loving God and Father: "He created us and redeemed us," i.e., past tense, for redemption has been accomplished in Christ, but Francis uses the future tense for God's saving activity, because we will be saved only if we freely accept God's mercy. Again, we respond to God's offer through the Son and in the Spirit, i.e., by a loving and personal relationship with Christ made possible by his Spirit. Just as the Father is made known to us and comes to us through the Son and Spirit, we return to the Father through the Son and Spirit. Bonaventure's metaphysical structure of reality of the *exitus* and *reductio* is found in Francis's consciousness: the movement is initiated *by* the Father and is *from* the Father and back *to* the Father. For Bonaventure it is expounded at length in the language of metaphysics; for Francis it is celebrated in the language of the Gospel.

In a beautiful prayer found in the *Earlier Rule*, Francis speaks directly to the Father *about* the Son in the third person in something akin to an anamnesis, or a "calling to mind" and presenting before the Father all Christ's redemptive work, together with the Holy Spirit's salvific activity.[153] He writes something similar in the *Later Admonition and Exhortation to the Brothers*

---

[152] *Earlier Rule* 23:8 in FAED 1, 84-85.
[153] *Earlier Rule* 23: 3-5 in FAED 1, 82-83. The anamnesis, properly speaking, is that part of the Eucharistic prayer which calls to mind Christ's Passion, Death, Resurrection, and Ascension, i.e., the Paschal Mystery. The Eucharistic prayer, as well as the liturgy as a whole, is an offering to the Father, through the Son, in the power of the Holy Spirit. See Leonard Lehmann, "'We Thank You:' The Structure and Content of Chapter 23 of the *Earlier Rule*," *Greyfriars Review* 5 (1991): 1-54.

and Sisters of Penance which is not a prayer addressed to God, but it reminds the faithful of the history of salvation, and connects it with the events of Holy Thursday (the Passover of the Lord) and the Paschal Mystery. It encourages the reception of the Eucharist with the proper disposition and the worship of the "Father in spirit and in truth" (John 4:23). As in the *Earlier Rule*, Francis proceeds to exhort the faithful repeatedly to love God "with all your heart and all your mind, and your neighbor as yourself" (Matt 22:37, 39).

Just as the foundations for Bonaventure's reflections may be found in Francis's acknowledgement of the primacy of the Father, so also Bonaventure reflects Francis's spiritual experience in its focus on the equality of the Son and Spirit with the Father and in eschewing any subordinationism in the Trinity. Francis states explicitly that the Three are equal when he says, "But because He is equal to the Father, the Son is not seen by anyone other than the Father or other than the Holy Spirit."[154] He is referring here to the Son's true and full divinity. Although Francis is known for his devotion to the humanity of Christ, and rightly so, Christ's humanity is not unduly emphasized. Francis is quite balanced in his writings when he expresses his understanding of the human and divine natures united in the Person of Christ, the hypostatic union. For Bonaventure the primacy of the Father does not imply preeminence or superiority or inequality, but ecstatic and infinite fecundity. For Francis the paternal primacy is simply where the biblical revelation begins, for Christ came to reveal the Father's overflowing love.

THE SON AS THE WORD AND CENTRAL PERSON OF THE TRINITY

God the Father dwells in inaccessible light, and is transcendent as the "Most High" and "Almighty Creator," yet Francis expresses a certain closeness and familiarity with God. When he calls God "Father," the "highest good," "love," "beauty," "security," "inner peace," "joy," "hope," and "our sweetness,"[155] he

---

[154] *Admonition* 1:7 in FAED 1, 128.
[155] *Praises of God* 4-6 in FAED 1, 109.

discloses something of a direct experience with the Transcendent. Almost every page of his writings offers us a glimpse of his profound, overwhelming, and sometimes ecstatic love for God. The sheer longing in his voice can be heard as Francis prays for his heart's desire: to be admitted to the Kingdom where:

> there is unclouded vision of You, perfect love of You, blessed companionship with You, eternal enjoyment of You.[156]

All that Francis knows of this God whom he loves with his very life and breath was disclosed through Christ. For Francis Christ is the fullest revelation of God, that is to say, he is God's Word. At one point he calls the Lord Jesus "the Word of the Father, and the words of the Holy Spirit."[157] Traditionally, we have understood the "Word of God" to mean that God's message and self-revelation in the history of salvation is a person, not a book, but a life lived among us who discloses at one and the same time who God is and who we are, or who we *can* be, as sons and daughters of the Father. To speak of the "words of the Holy Spirit" is unusual, but Jesus did offer us a divine message in the form of literal words, inspired by the Spirit. Jesus assured his disciples not to be anxious about what they would reply to hostile authorities, because "what you are to say will be given to you in that hour; for it is not you who speak, but the Spirit of your Father speaking through you" (Matt 10:19b-20; Mark 13:11; Luke 12:11-12). The Spirit has a prophetic role as well as the Son.

Francis's quote from John's Gospel in his First Admonition demonstrates his understanding of the Son's role in relation to the Father:

> The Lord Jesus says to His disciples: "I am the way, the truth and the life; No one comes to the Father except through me. If you knew me, you would also know my Father; and from now on, you do know him and have

---

[156] *Our Father* 4 in FAED 1, 158.
[157] *Later Admonition* 3 in FAED 1, 45.

seen him ... Whoever sees me, sees my Father as well (John 14:6-9).[158]

The Son is quite simply Francis's personal Way to the Father, a trinitarian theology "from below." In Bonaventure's terms, the Son is the *persona media*, through whom we encounter God's inexhaustible love and through whom we respond to that love. In that sense, Christ is central, the personal means to God. In Bonaventure's theology, the Son is the Central Person of the Trinity, the Word through whom[159] the Father creates the universe, reveals Godself to us, redeems and saves us, and through whom we respond to the Father. Without alluding to the exemplarity we find prominently in Bonaventure, Francis portrays the Son as the central person in the *exitus* and *reductio*. When Francis speaks of the Son, he does so in context of the Trinity. Christ is the true and "beloved Son"[160] whose will is at one with the Father's will. He is also the "true Light" and "Wisdom of the Father" who imparts spiritual wisdom to believers.[161] It is an unambiguously Scriptural and functional Christology: Francis tells us what Christ did for our redemption: the Incarnation, the Passion and Death.[162].

Oddly, Francis does not mention the Resurrection often in his writings, although in the *Earlier Rule* he does thank the Father for the Son's second coming.[163] Francis's discussion of Christ is centered on this functional Christology and on Gospel quotations of Christ's teachings such as to love God and neighbor. It seems that all Francis ever needed to say about Christ

---

[158] *Admonition* 1:1-4 in FAED 1, 128.

[159] *Later Admonition* 3, 4 and 12; *Earlier Rule* 23:1, 3 in FAED 1, 45-46; 81-82.

[160] "True Son" in *Admonition* 1:8; "Beloved Son" in *Admonition* 5:1; in *Earlier Rule*, 23:5, 6; in *Letter to the Entire Order* 51; and in *A Salutation of the Blessed Virgin Mary* 2 in FAED 1, 128; 131; 82-83; 120-21; 163.

[161] *Later Admonition* 66-67 in FAED 1, 50.

[162] See Thaddée Matura, "'My Holy Father!' God as Father in the Writings of St. Francis," *Greyfriars Review* 1 (1987): 105-30.

[163] *Earlier Rule* 23:4 in FAED 1, 82.

was said in the way he lived his own life, in following perfectly "in the footprints of [the] Beloved Son."[164]

This is especially true with regard to the quintessential Franciscan virtue of humility which Francis learned from Christ and which he embodied in his own life. The Incarnation was an event of infinite and ineffable divine condescension. Francis sees the utter humility of the Beloved Son of the Most High who "came from the royal throne into the Virgin's womb,"[165] and shared in "our humanity and frailty."[166] But it was not only our humanity that he chose, it was also a lowly and humble estate. "Though He was rich (2 Cor 8:9), He wished, together with … His mother to choose poverty in the world beyond all else."[167] The Son is God,[168] equal to the Father,[169] abides eternally in the intimate and loving communion of the "perfect Trinity and simple Unity,"[170] and yet the Son became incarnate to know suffering as humans know suffering. Jesus experienced deprivation, hunger, thirst, oppression, betrayal, abandonment, false accusation, condemnation, brutalization, torture, humiliation, crucifixion, and an ignoble death. Francis does not describe the suffering of Christ to any length, but no one, except for an eyewitness to the events, could know Christ's sufferings more than Francis.

THE TRINITY AND THE EUCHARIST

For Francis the revelation of the Trinity is first and foremost a revelation that God is a *communion* of love. The Father, Son, and Spirit eternally abide in loving relationships, with a love so unfathomably deep, that it is unitive and ecstatic at the same time; divine love makes them one and overflows into each oth-

---

[164] *Entire Order* 51 in FAED 1, 120.
[165] *Admonition* 1:16 in FAED 1, 129.
[166] *Later Admonition* 4 in FAED 1, 46.
[167] *Later Admonition* 4 in FAED 1, 46.
[168] *Admonition* 1:20 in FAED 1, 129.
[169] *Admonition* 1:7 in FAED 1, 128.
[170] *Letter to the Entire Order* 52; cf. also: *Earlier Rule*, 21:2; 23:11; 24:2; *Exhortation to the Praise of God* 16 in FAED 1, 121; 78; 85-86; 86; 138.

er, and beyond themselves to human beings. Divine love becomes fully human in Christ, and is ultimately made manifest in his passion and cross. Throughout the centuries, the Eucharist is the Church's commemoration and "making present" of Christ's passion, death, and resurrection. Francis experiences the Eucharist as the living and real presence of Christ, for he says, "… let us, as we see bread and wine with our bodily eyes, see and firmly believe that they are His most holy Body and Blood living and true. And in this way the Lord is always with His faithful, as He Himself says: 'Behold I am with you until the end of the age.'"[171] Although Francis does not use these words, the Eucharist is the most sacred and solemn invitation to enter into *communion* of love with Christ.

Francis is unique in connecting the Eucharist with the Trinity. It is a subtle connection, but a perceptible one nevertheless, as we can see from one example in his *Admonitions*. He begins *The Admonitions* by reminding us of the inaccessibility of the Father, the Incarnation of the Son who reveals the Father, and the empowering role of the Holy Spirit. This is evidence of a trinitarian consciousness. He then immediately starts to speak of the Eucharist, exhorting us to have a proper disposition for receiving the sacrament.[172] There is a logic at work here: Francis rarely discusses the Person of Christ, except in relation to his Father or in the context of the Trinity. For Francis the Father dwells in inaccessible light, and the Word and Beloved Son became incarnate, to show us the way to the Father and to show us the Father. "… no one comes to the Father except through me. If you had known me, you would also have known my Father … whoever sees me, sees also my Father" (John 14:6-9). Yet, Francis explains, not all who saw Christ according to his humanity saw the Father, nor did they believe that he was the true Son of God. And now in a similar way, not all those who see the Eucharist see and believe that it is the Body and Blood of Christ. It is by the Holy Spirit that we accept this.[173]

---

[171] *Admonition* 1:21-22 in FAED 1, 129.
[172] *Admonition* 1:1-13; see also *Later Admonition* 4-22 in FAED 1, 128-29; 46-47.
[173] *Admonition* 1:12-13 in FAED 1, 129.

Francis reminds us that Christ humbled himself for our redemption, but by including the Father and Spirit in this context, Francis also reminds us that our redemption is found not only in Christ's cross, but also in his revealing the Father, in his revealing the Father's love for him and for us, and also in his pouring out the Spirit to empower us to believe. When Francis speaks of Christ, often the whole Trinity is invoked or called to mind, even in relation to the Eucharist which may seem as the sacrament uniquely identified with Christ. Our redemption is the work of the whole Trinity.

In the *Admonitions* Francis is not trying to present an exposition of trinitarian theology and the Eucharist. I see his connection of the Trinity and the Eucharist merely as evidence of an abiding trinitarian "consciousness" in his relationship with God. Clearly, Francis's intent is to encourage us to believe in the true and living presence of Christ in the Eucharist and to exhort us to receive him worthily. When Francis recounts the divine condescension for our salvation, he is appealing to our emotions, to our sense of compassion and gratitude. He wants us to believe humbly that Christ is not "gone," not "reabsorbed" into the Trinity, so to speak, but is alive, "accessible," and still seeking to give himself to us in the Eucharist. Francis's trinitarian theology "from below" views the Eucharist as communion of love with the Incarnate and Crucified Christ.

The Eucharist is an enduring extension of the divine condescension God displayed in the incarnation and the redemption. In the Real Presence, Christ makes himself humble in giving himself to us as our food and spiritual sustenance. Francis makes this stunningly clear in the following quotation from his *Letter to the Entire Order*:

> Let everyone be struck with fear,
> Let the whole world tremble,
> and let the heavens exult
> when Christ, the Son of the living God,
> is present on the altar in the hands of a priest!
> O wonderful loftiness and stupendous dignity!
> O sublime humility!

> O humble sublimity!
> That the Lord of the universe,
> God and the Son of God,
> so humbles Himself
> that for our salvation
> He hides Himself
> under an ordinary piece of bread!
> Brothers, look at the humility of God,
> and pour out your hearts before Him!
> Humble yourselves that you may be exalted by Him![174]

In the Eucharist the Paschal Mystery, that is Christ's passion, death, and resurrection, is called to mind and "made present," and we enter into these redemptive events ritually, symbolically, and sacramentally. Francis is reminding the Order, first, of the divine self-emptying for our sakes in the redemption and second, in the Eucharist which makes it present and accessible to us daily.

THE HOLY SPIRIT: OUR INSPIRATION AND UNITY

Ever-present and as necessary as the air we breathe, the Holy Spirit is, nevertheless, the subtle Person of the Trinity. It is the life-giving Spirit who moves us to open our hearts to Christ's message and follow him to the Father. Francis understands clearly the powerful role of the Spirit[175] in his life, as we can deduce from the approximately twenty references to the Spirit in his writings.

Francis's relationship with God is through the Son, but it is the Spirit at work in him to open his eyes to who Christ is and to how infinitely God loves us in Christ. Francis admonishes us to remember that, just as the Son reveals God the Father who dwells in inaccessible light, it is the Holy Spirit who allows us to see that Christ is God the Son. It is the Spirit who opens icy

---

[174] *Letter to the Entire Order* 26-28 in FAED 1, 118.
[175] See Optatus van Asseldonk, "The Spirit of the Lord and Its Holy Activity in the Writings of Francis," *Greyfriars Review* 5 (1991): 103-58.

hearts to believe in Christ and to accept God's love. As Francis noted in his *First Admonition*, not all those who saw Jesus in his lifetime, "according to His humanity," saw and believed that He was the true Son of God, unless they "saw and believed according to the Spirit."[176] This is an extraordinary and very appropriate way to begin a set of Admonitions: It is trinitarian; it presents the traditional Christian way to God—through Christ and in the Spirit; and it makes Christ the central focus of the faith, without neglecting the role of the Spirit in our coming to God.

Francis quotes Paul the Apostle in saying that, "No one can say 'Jesus is Lord' except in the Holy Spirit" (I Cor 12:3).[177] The Holy Spirit gives the gift of faith. To say that faith is a gift is to say that it is not earned, achieved, or awarded. It is freely given and it must be freely accepted, because faith is essentially a relationship with God. Loving and meaningful relationships in our lives cannot be earned, achieved, or awarded. In such a relationship another person's love is simply and freely bestowed on us. Francis uses the term "the Spirit of the Lord," i.e., the Spirit of the Lord Jesus, as Paul used the designation for the Third Person of the Trinity.[178] Therefore it is clear that the Spirit is the Spirit of both the Father and the Son. Francis also calls the Spirit the Paraclete (the Comforter).[179]

The Holy Spirit is God ever-present in the universe, permeating all reality with energy, life, love, and movement towards a good purpose. God's presence through the Spirit gives life, understanding, unity, and meaning to the Christian life, and can set our hearts aflame in the fire of divine love, so that we may love God through Christ and our neighbors as ourselves. He admonishes his brothers to seek above all else the Holy Spirit's "holy activity" in their lives.[180] Francis is exceedingly open to the Spirit's "holy activity" in his own life. He is conscious that it

---

[176] *Admonition* 1:5-8 in FAED 1, 128.

[177] *Admonition* 8:1 in FAED 1, 132.

[178] Rom 8:9; Phil 1:19; Gal 4:6.

[179] *Earlier Rule* 23:5; *Entire Order* 33; *Salutation to Mary* 2; *The Testament* 40 in FAED 1, 82-83; 119; 163; 127.

[180] *Later Rule* 10:8; also *Earlier Admonition* 1:10 and 2:21; *Later Admonition* 53 in FAED 1, 105; 42, 44; 49.

is the Third Person of the Trinity who allows him to "see and believe" that Christ is the Son of God who reveals the Father. The Spirit is a dynamic presence: The Spirit "lives in His faithful;"[181] enlightens us to "see and believe" in Christ;[182] allows us to receive the Eucharist more worthily;[183] moves us to prayer and devotion;[184] inspires self-denial;[185] makes us "children of the heavenly Father" whose work we do;[186] and inwardly cleanses, enlightens, and inflames us to be "able to follow in the footprints of ... our Lord Jesus Christ."[187] In the *Major Legend* Bonaventure was right to depict Francis acting under the welcome inspiration of the Spirit. While there is no way anyone could know when and where the Spirit moved Francis, Bonaventure's accounts are representative of Francis's experience of the Spirit and of his articulation of this experience in his writings.

How does one know whether the Spirit of the Lord is operative in one's life? There is tremendous wisdom in Francis's answer when he says the Spirit's presence may be recognized "if his flesh does not pride itself [when] the Lord performs some good through him, ... his flesh does not therefore exalt itself ... Instead he regards himself the more worthless and esteems himself less than all others."[188] The mark of the Spirit is doing good humbly.

It is thoroughly consistent in the Franciscan consciousness to connect an understanding of the Spirit's activity with humility. The depth of divine self-emptying and humility is exemplified not only in the Son's assuming human flesh with all its frailty, and not only in his suffering an excruciating death, but also in his coming down daily in a humble form; "each day He comes down from the bosom of the Father ... in the hands of the priest."[189] In imitating our Lord Jesus, the Holy Spirit inspires

---

[181] *Admonition* 1:12 in FAED 1, 129.
[182] *Admonition* 1:8 in FAED 1, 128.
[183] *Admonition* 1:9 in FAED 1, 128.
[184] *Later Rule* 5:2 in FAED 1, 102.
[185] *Earlier Rule* 17:14 in FAED 1, 75.
[186] *Later Admonition* 49 in FAED 1, 48-49.
[187] *Entire Order* 51 in FAED 1, 120-21.
[188] *Admonition* 12:1-3 in FAED 1, 133.
[189] *Admonition* 1:17-18 in FAED 1, 129.

genuine humility in us to do the work of the Father without pride, just as Jesus did. It is not a true self-emptying if we become full of pride. The Paraclete spurs us to strip away egoism and spiritual pride, and to do good for its own sake, for the sake of the recipient, and for the love of God. Francis knows it is no achievement to say, "Jesus is Lord," or to live as humbly as Christ, or to do good and the work of the Father, "except in the Holy Spirit" (1 Cor 12:3)[190] because it is all "gift." It is all freely and generously given to us in the Spirit, if only we would accept it.

The most original articulation of the Spirit's activity is found in the *Earlier Exhortation* and the *Later Admonition and Exhortation* in which Francis speaks metaphorically about our relationship with the Father, the Son, and the Spirit, but places these relationships within the purview of the Spirit. He begins the *Earlier Exhortation* with the evangelical command to love God above all (Mark 12:30) and our neighbors as ourselves (Matt 22:39), to repent, and to receive the Eucharist worthily, i.e., a concise summation of the Christian life. Such Christians are "happy and blessed,"

> … because the Spirit of the Lord will rest upon them and make [His] home and dwelling place among them, and they are children of the heavenly Father Whose works they do, and they are spouses, brothers, and mothers of our Lord Jesus Christ. We are spouses when the faithful soul is joined by the Holy Spirit to our Lord Jesus Christ. We are brothers to Him when we do the will of the Father Who is in heaven. We are mothers when we carry Him in our heart and body through a divine love and a pure and sincere conscience and give birth to Him through a holy activity which must shine as an example before others.[191]

---

[190] See Francis's references to the action of the Spirit in the *Earlier Rule* 17:9-16 in FAED 1, 75-76 (with its references to Rom 8:6).

[191] *Earlier Exhortation* 1:6-10; cf. *Later Admonition* 48-53, in FAED 1, 41-42; 48-49.

God is all about relationship because God is all about love. We speak of God as Father, Son, and Spirit because these metaphors reveal an often elusive truth about God's mode of existence as a loving, inter-Personal communion. We call God Father as Jesus taught us, but many other relational metaphors may express an experience of God's personal encounter with us. This is patently true regarding Francis's choice of relational metaphors in the quotation above.

The metaphors are placed within the context of the Spirit's activity of coming to "rest upon" and of making "His home and dwelling among" the faithful in order to make them "children of the heavenly Father"—the first relationship mentioned. This relational metaphor is so common in Scripture and among Christians that it would normally go unnoticed. It is uniquely and distinctly the role of the Spirit to unify God and human beings in a new relationship through Christ, both in salvation history and in each individual's life.

In speculative trinitarian theology the Spirit has a uniquely unitive role within the inner life of the Trinity as being the mutual Gift and Bond of Love between the Father and the Son. While Francis does not use these traditional titles of the Spirit, he does have a deep intuition of the Paraclete's unitive and dynamic role in incorporating us into divine communion expressed as some human relational metaphor. Thus, Christians are not only "children of the Father" whose work we do, but also brothers and sisters of Christ when we do the will of His Father.

Again like "children of the Father," this relationship of being "Christ's brothers and sisters" is not uncommon. However, the other two relationships mentioned in the quote above, "spouses" and "mothers" of Christ, while not unheard of, are more rare. Francis states:

> We are spouses when the faithful soul is joined by the Holy Spirit to our Lord Christ.... We are mothers when we carry Him in our heart and body through divine love

and a pure and sincere conscience and we give birth to Him …[192]

Francis is trying to convey the kind of deeply loving and intimate relationship that is possible with Christ through the dynamic and unitive activity of the Holy Spirit. Spousal love is freely chosen, faithful, exclusive, unitive, life-giving, and totally self-giving. Unlike a father, mother, and brother, one *chooses* a spouse and freely consents to the relationship. One chooses also to be faithful and committed exclusively to one's spouse as the center of one's life. Human spouses unite everything they have and everything they are because of their love: they unite their fortunes, their property, their dreams and aspirations, and their futures. The spouses' ideal of mutual self-giving is total: it is a commitment towards lifelong self-giving symbolized in an actual and physical giving of self in sexual intimacy.

Similarly, the mother-child relationship is a unique kind of love that is characterized by profound self-giving and self-sacrificing care and attention. It is a love that is possible with Christ through the unitive activity of the Spirit. It is the kind of love that is literally borne in one's body with all the sacrifices and pain that entails, including the labor necessary in delivery.

Francis is trying to describe the experience he has had of God's love. It is multi-dimensional, all-encompassing, and joyous. It is trinitarian! He allows himself an outburst of emotion right after his descriptions in saying,

> O how glorious it is to have a holy and great Father in heaven! O how holy, consoling to have such a beautiful and wonderful Spouse! O how holy and how loving, gratifying, humbling, peace-giving, sweet, worthy of love, and, above all things, desirable: to have such a Brother and such a Son, our Lord Jesus Christ…[193]

This section, found in both documents, which describes familial relationships with Christ by the power of the Spirit is fol-

---

[192] *Earlier Exhortation* 1:8, 10; *Later Admonition* 51, 53 in FAED 1, 42; 49.
[193] *Earlier Exhortation*, 1:11 in FAED 1, 42.

lowed by selected lines from Jesus' intimate prayer to his Father in John's Gospel (John 17:8-24). Jesus prays that his disciples may be protected, blessed and sanctified, and especially that "they may be sanctified *in being one* (John 17:23) *as we are one* (John 17:11)" ... so that "where I am, they may be with me ..."[194] In quoting Christ's prayer for unity, Francis is alluding to the possibility that each Christian is offered, which is to enter into the very communion that the Father and Son share. By situating the Johannine quotation in the context of the Spirit's unitive action, Francis is suggesting that this offering of divine life is by the power of Spirit.

Conclusion:
Francis's Experience of the tri-Personal God

Francis does not speculate about the Trinity; he does not use the language of philosophy to understand the faith. Therefore theologians would seriously hesitate to call his writings on the Trinity "theology."[195] Whether it is "monastic theology" or "university theology," the term has not been applied to Francis's writings, for he was neither a learned monastic nor a professional academic. Yet, rarely has any theologian written about the Trinity so movingly and compellingly, so beautifully and convincingly, so lucidly and joyfully, than this simple lover of God. This is especially true of his emotion-filled prayers addressed as a son to the Father, through the Son and with the Son, in the power of the Spirit. Francis's writings may be characterized as a "trinitarian theology from below," where God met him.

---

[194] *Earlier Exhortation*, 1:11-13; cf. *Later Admonition*, 54-56 in FAED 1, 42; 49. Emphasis added to the Johannine quotation.

[195] Bernard McGinn characterizes such religious writing as "vernacular theology" in *The Flowering of Mysticism: Men and Women in the New Mysticism—1200-1350* (New York: Crossroad, 1998), 18-24. For an excellent discussion on Francis as a "vernacular theologian," see Dominic Monti, "Francis as Vernacular Theologian: A Link to the Franciscan Intellectual Tradition," *The Franciscan Intellectual Tradition:* Washington Theological Union Symposium Papers 2001, ed. Elise Saggau (St. Bonaventure, NY: Franciscan Institute Publications, 2002), 21-42.

Francis's experience of God as Trinity is transformative. It moves him to minister to lepers, the sick, and the suffering; to console the spiritually troubled; to give alms to the poor; to preach penitence and to give witness to the Gospel in every moment of every day of his life. Francis "follows in Christ's footprints" and abandons any opportunity for wealth, a family, and all that one would think would make a man legitimately happy in this world. As the son of a cloth seller, Francis could have had a good future as a merchant; he could have fallen in love, raised a family, and contributed as a valued member of the Assisi community. He could have lived such a life devoted to God as a deeply religious Christian. But Francis's love for God is dynamic, ecstatic, overwhelming, and all-consuming. The man was deeply and passionately in love with God. His *Prayer Inspired by the Our Father* reveals his heart's desire, but not just for himself. He speaks in the first person plural, desiring the highest Good for others as he did for himself:

> That we may love You with our whole heart by always thinking of You, with our whole soul by always desiring You, with our whole mind by always directing all our intentions to You, and by seeking Your glory in everything, and with all our strength by exerting all our energies and affections of body and soul in the service of Your love and of nothing else; and may we love our neighbors as ourselves ...[196]

As a direct heir of Francis's spiritual experience, as a leader of the Franciscan family, as a theologian of the University, Bonaventure tried to capture Francis's experience for the Church and society of his time through the use of the tools of philosophy and academic theology. We have seen some of the implications of his reflections. Francis accorded a certain primacy to the Father, but, as we have seen, this primacy can in no way be construed as preeminence, but as inexhaustible Self-emptying love which eternally begets the Son. Bonaventure developed

---

[196] *Our Father*, 5 in FAED 1, 158-59.

Francis's insight further by positing that primacy is divine fecundity. Both hold Christ to be the Central Person of the Trinity and made Christ the center of their lives, following in his footsteps to the Father. Both were conscious of the Holy Spirit's unitive and empowering role. Both lived according to an *"exitus* and *reductio* worldview"; knowing that all reality (both divine and created) comes from the Father and returns to the Father through Christ and in the Spirit.

Bonaventure tried to fashion a community in its personal, fraternal, and missionary life around this central experience of Trinitarian life through his *Major Legend* of Francis. The indisputable Franciscan insight in our understanding of the Trinity is the inexhaustible and overwhelming love God has for us. Others have written about divine love at the center of the Trinity, but in the Franciscan consciousness, love is more prominent and more permeating. Love in the Franciscan cast reveals itself in divine kenosis (self-emptying), humility, and condescension. God seeks to unite us in self-transcending divine communion. And finally the contemplation of the Trinity in the Franciscan Tradition causes unabashed joy and exuberance.

SELECTED BIBLIOGRAPHY

Bonaventure. *The Breviloquium*. Ed. and trans. by Dominic V. Monti, Works of St. Bonaventure Vol. IX. St. Bonaventure, NY: Franciscan Institute Publications, 2005.

_____. *The Collations on the Six Days*. In *The Works of Bonaventure*. Vol. V. Trans. by Jose de Vinck. Paterson, NJ: St. Anthony Guild Press, 1970.

_____. *The Major Legend of Saint Francis* (*The Life of Blessed Francis*). In *Francis of Assisi: Early Documents*, Vol. II: *The Founder*. Ed. by Regis J. Armstrong, J.A. Wayne Hellman, and William J. Short. Hyde Park, NY: New City Press, 2000.

_____. *Disputed Questions on the Mystery of the Trinity*. Trans. by Zachary Hayes, Works of St. Bonaventure Vol. III. St. Bonaventure, NY: The Franciscan Institute, 1979.

_____. *The Soul's Journey into God*. In *Itinerarium Mentis in Deum*. Trans by Philotheus Boehner and Zachary Hayes, Works of St. Bonaventure Vol. II. St. Bonaventure, NY: Franciscan Institute Publications, 2002.

Calisi, Maria. "Bonaventure's Trinity: Revelation of an Intensely Personal God," *The Cord* Vol. 51, No. 3 (May/June 2001): 125-37.

_____. "Bonaventure's Trinitarian Theology as a Feminist Resource," *Spirit and Life: A Journal of Contemporary Franciscanism* Vol. 8 (1999): 117-32.

Cousins, Ewert. *Bonaventure and the Coincidence of Opposites*. Chicago: Franciscan Herald Press, 1978.

_____. "A Theology of Interpersonal Relations." *Thought* 45 (1970): 56-82.

Francesco d'Assisi, *Scritti, Testo latino e traduzione italiana*. Milano: Editrici Francescane, 2002.

Hayes, Zachary. "Bonaventure: Mystery of the Triune God." In *The History of Franciscan Theology*. Edited by Kenan B. Osborne. St. Bonaventure, NY: The Franciscan Institute, 1994, 39-125.

———. "Bonaventure of Bagnoregio: A Paradigm for Franciscan Theologians?" In *The Franciscan Intellectual Tradition: Washington Theological Union Symposium Papers 2001*. St. Bonaventure, NY: Franciscan Institute Publications, 2002: 43-56.

———. "Christology and Metaphysics in the Thought of Bonaventure." In *Celebrating the Medieval Heritage: A Colloquy on the Thought of Aquinas and Bonaventure*. Edited by David Tracy. The Journal of Religion 58 (Supplement 1978): S82-S96.

———. *The Hidden Center: Spirituality and Speculative Christology in St. Bonaventure*. New York: Paulist Press, 1981.

———. "Incarnation and Creation in the Theology of St. Bonaventure." *Studies Honoring Ignatius C. Brady*. Edited by R. Almagno, 1976, 309-29.

LaCugna, Catherine Mowry. *God For Us: The Trinity and Christian Life*. HarperSanFrancisco, 1991.

Lehmann, Leonard. "'We Thank You:' The Structure and Content of Chapter 23 of the *Earlier Rule*." *Greyfriars Review* 5 (1991): 1-54.

Matura, Thaddée. *Francis of Assisi: The Message in His Writings*. Translated by Paul Barrett. St. Bonaventure, NY: The Franciscan Institute, 1997.

———."'My Holy Father!' God as Father in the Writings of St. Francis." *Greyfriars Review* 1 (September, 1987): 105-30.

McGinn, Bernard. *The Flowering of Mysticism: Men and Women in the New Mysticism—1200-1350*. Vol. III of The Presence of God: A History of Western Christian Mysticism. New York: Crossroad, 1998.

Miccoli, Giovanni. "The Writings of Francis," *Greyfriars Review* 15 (2001): 135-70.

Monti, Dominic. "Francis as Vernacular Theologian: A Link to the Franciscan Intellectual Tradition?" In *The Franciscan Intellectual Tradition: Washington Theological Union Symposium Papers 2001*. St. Bonaventure, NY: The Franciscan Institute, 2002: 21-42.

Nguyen-Van-Khanh, Norbert. *The Teacher of His Heart: Jesus Christ in the Thought and Writings of St. Francis*. Translated by Ed Hagman. St. Bonaventure, NY: The Franciscan Institute, 1994.

Paolazzi, Carlo. "Francis and His Use of Scribes: A Puzzle to Scholars," *Greyfriars Review* 18 (2004): 323-41.

Van Asseldonk, Optatus. "The Spirit of the Lord and Its Holy Activity in the Writings of Francis." *Greyfriars Review* 5 (1991): 103-58.